# THE
# TACTICS
# OF
# PRESSURE

A critical review of six
British pressure groups

Edited by
## Brian Frost

1975

GALLIARD
LONDON: STAINER & BELL LTD

SBN 85249 311 8
Stainer & Bell Ltd, 82 High Road, London N2 9PW
Printed in England by Galliard Ltd

# CONTENTS

# CONTRIBUTORS

**Brian Frost** is Programme Director of the London Ecumenical Centre, a centre in London concerned with city problems. Before that he was a member of the staff of the Christian Aid Department of the British Council of Churches.

**Andrew Colman** gained two degrees in psychology at the University of Capetown, and lectured at Capetown and Rhodes before taking up his present post as Lecturer in Psychology at the University of Leicester.

**Judith Young**, now working in a tax office in Blackburn, received a distinction at the University of Manchester for a thesis on the Aid Lobby in Britain.

**Antony Grey** was the director of the Albany Trust and Secretary of the Homosexual Law Reform Society.

**Ian Henderson**, ordained on the Southwark Ordination Course, was responsible for the setting up of a hostel for homeless women when he worked for Christian Action. He was one of the Trustees of Shelter, subsequently joining the United Nations Association as Secretary. He has also worked for the Disablement Income Group and the Elfrida Rathbone Society.

**John Flewin** works for the Three Counties News Agency and was the PRO for the Wing Resistance Group formed to oppose the siting of the third London airport at Cublington.

**Barbara McCallum** is a social worker with a London Borough. Before that she was a member of the Port Harcourt Team Ministry and on her return to Britain was involved in the Biafra Lobby.

**William Wallace** works for the Department of Government of Manchester University in the Faculty of Economic and Social Studies. He has been a Liberal candidate and at the moment is working on the role of pressure groups in British Foreign Policy.

# INTRODUCTION

When at the Notting Hill Ecumenical Centre* I sponsored a day's consultation on pressure groups to see if there was anything which different pressure groups could learn from each other and if any further action was needed in this area in Britain.

Several ideas were floated by the end of the day by a diverse number of people with experience in the pressure group world. One was the need for an ABC of UK pressure groups. Another was the need for a change in the laws of charity in order to bring them up to date with present-day needs. A third was a critical look at a number of pressure groups, to see why they were successful, or unsuccessful, and to examine the different kinds of approach used by a number of very varied groups.

This is the genesis of the book *The Tactics of Pressure*. The groups written about have been chosen because they are representative of a number of areas of concern in contemporary Britain.

The Aid Lobby has been chosen because it is concerned with an issue which is global, but which has received considerable local support throughout the United Kingdom. It is also a pressure group which cannot point to any end success, being involved in a massive attempt to alter existing imbalance in the world today. In some measure it has succeeded in short-term aims, but in the long run, though it has made aid fashionable, how can it affect policies of governmental action at an international level? That is the unresolved problem.

The question of homosexual law reform has been chosen because it stands for a number of issues which have found a pivotal point in the Council for Civil Liberties. It has also been successful in part and points to the fact that even an inherently unpopular subject can be talked about and campaigned for. In addition, it shows clearly the inner workings of Parliament and cautions against a too-optimistic interpretation by pressure group supporters of their efficacy.

There are a number of associations which in a sense contain pressure group work but are really movements rather than pressure groups. Shelter is one of these, and the pressure-group side of its work has been considered not only because it is so well known but also because in a way, by its use of high-pressure

* Now incorporated in the London Ecumenical Centre.

advertising, it broke out of a certain mould within which many similar groups had operated.

Many groups, of course, fail; it is worth examining the reasons for this, however correct and right their cause. The Biafra Lobby has been included for this reason; again, because it pinpoints the difficulty of the work of a pressure group within Britain which aims to alter something in another part of the world. It also brings to light the different kinds of alliances which occur from time to time, both in favour of pressure on a certain point and against it. It is interesting to reflect on the comparative success in the short term of the Angola Action Group compared with the impotence of the Biafra Lobby, despite its being so well-informed.

Environmental issues seem to be coming to the fore more and more as points of pressure in Britain. Some think that such pressure groups are right-wing and the emergence of a new form of middle-class pressure for its own selfish ends. It would be informative to have included a group like the arms lobby on South Africa, to see such a middle-class lobby in action, but this has proved extremely difficult to document.

Another way of of handling the environment issue would have been to look at the Motorway Development Trust in Kensington, to see how a community pressure group reacted to the extension of the M4. But we have chosen the siting of the Third London Airport as an issue worthy of a closer look because, though affecting only a certain area and a certain number of people, it does show how over a short period of time a highly articulate group and alliance was created. In what way it could be emulated on other environmental issues is not clear. It certainly involved a large number of people in pressure group work in a new way.

The final pressure group considered is one which has been substantially successful, even quoted with approbation by ministers in two governments—DIG, the Disablement Income Group. It stands for any number of pressure groups concerned with the human needs of a specific group of deprived and ignored people.

At the end of the book there is a long article by William Wallace, of the Department of Government at The University of Manchester, on the phenomenon of pressure groups. I thought it better that his essay should appear at the end, by which time the readers have had a chance to react to the groups described, than at the beginning.

The book begins with Andrew Colman's article on the

psychology of influence. This complements the final article, and sets the scene for the discussion of the individual pressure groups, by exploring the motivation of those people who engage in pressure group activity.

It is, I think, clear that pressure group activity will grow rather than diminish. Mr Wallace's assessment, together with the descriptions of the work of the six groups, provides data for a critical assessment of what are appropriate tactics of pressure.

Brian Frost
London Ecumenical Centre

# THE PSYCHOLOGY OF INFLUENCE
## ANDREW COLMAN

Pressure groups are viewed by many contemporary political theorists as desirable or even indispensible instruments for the defence and promotion of liberty and justice in modern industrial democracies. The case has been argued most zealously by S. E. Finer in *The Anonymous Empire* (Pall Mall, 1966) and by S. M. Lipset, W. Kornhauser and others in their various writings on 'pluralism'. It has been suggested, furthermore, that the various pressure groups in present day Britain collectively embody an informal representative system of possibly greater importance than the formal representation built into our parliamentary structure (S. H. Beer, *Modern British Politics,* Faber, 1965).

The favourable public image enjoyed by pressure groups today stands in sharp contrast to the abhorrence and apprehension with which they were viewed by Rousseau and most philosophers of the classical liberal tradition, who considered the organized pursuit of sectional or vested interests to be inherently conspiratorial and inimical to the public interest. According to that tradition, citizens should be encouraged to follow their various self-interested ends as individuals, and the state should be conceived as the embodiment of their collective will.

The growth in scale and complexity of the governmental process which followed in the wake of the industrial revolution led on the one hand to an inevitable erosion of this individualistic conception of democracy, and on the other to an ever-increasing celebration of pressure groups. It led also to what R. P. Wolff has described, in *A Critique of Pure Tolerance* (Cape, 1969), as the modern 'vector-sum' conception of democracy, which views the government as a pivotal point of forces exerted on it by pressure groups throughout the nation, its function being to resolve these conflicting forces into a single balanced policy. As the relative weights of the various groups change, the fulcrum of government swings about, in sympathy with the drift of public opinion. Instead of being jostled by a bewildering array of inarticulate private citizens, the government can weigh up the various interests of a manageable and clearly distinguishable set of organized pressure groups, in which all significant interests in the nation are represented, and dispense political, social and economic goodies to each in rough proportion to its relative size and intensity.

The fact that the British government does not actually reach decisions in this manner is aptly illustrated by the refusal of successive Home Secretaries in recent years to re-introduce capital punishment for crimes other than treason, despite the relative size and intensity of the pro-hanging lobby. The reason for this is that human actions (including those of Home Secretaries) are often motivated by principles rather than interests. R. P. Wolff has pointed out that the 'vector-sum' conception of democracy is premised on the possibility and desirability of compromise or give-and-take, which is wholly inappropriate in matters of principle, when opposing views are indivisible and cannot be resolved by a process of distributive justice, and each side claims universal validity for its point of view. One of the fallacies of the 'vector-sum' conception resides, therefore, in the psychologically naive theory of human motivation and decision-making, a relic of the discredited Utilitarianism of Bentham and J. S. Mill, which lurks behind it, and which views all human action as motivated by interests. It is, nevertheless, true that compromise between conflicting interest groups does frequently form the basis of government decisions, and what many people consider to be matters of principle are sometimes treated as though they were simply conflicts of interest. The constraints on the BBC to balance programmes which promote controversial points of view with programmes promoting 'the other side' frequently result in frustration and anger among sections of the viewing and listening public for this reason. Access programmes such as *Open Door*, in which groups promoting sense and nonsense, progressive and reactionary views, truth and falsehood are given equal exposure, treated with equal seriousness and thus reduced to a common denominator, evoke similar reactions among those who believe that the right to access cannot be ethically decided upon as if it were purely a matter of distributive justice.

In practice, a pressure group in Britain usually finds itself confronted by a more or less principled government policy on the issue at hand, and its task is to influence the decision-makers to change that policy. This in turn usually involves inducing them either to modify the principles which guide their existing policy, or to modify the policy in spite of the principles, in the interests of expediency for example. The former course is open to any pressure group, and involves an exercise in persuasive attitude change directed at the decision-makers or the public at large. The latter, which is more frequently successful, is available only to groups which possess some measure of power over the government through, for example, their control over resources which the government depends upon, and involves an exercise in bargaining. These are, of course, ideal types, and numerous finer distinctions could be made. It would be reasonable, however, to characterise the Homosexual Law Reform Society as a typical persuasive pressure group, and the trade unions, in so far as they attempt to influence government policy, as typical bargaining pressure groups. In general, interest groups which represent clearly identifiable sections of society, such as the National Union of Mineworkers, the Provisional IRA, or the British Medical Association, tend more often to be able to engage in genuine bargaining than do purely promotional or cause groups which do not speak for any specific interest other than society at large, such as the Campaign for Nuclear Disarmament, the Aid Lobby or the Friends of the Earth.

In what follows, an attempt will be made to summarise some of the more significant findings to have emerged from psychological research on attitude change and persuasion in so far as they bear on the concrete situations in which pressure groups typically find themselves, and an outline will then be given of the strategy of bargaining as it has been elucidated by informal game theory. The process of attitude change has attracted an enormous amount of attention from research workers, and constitutes one of the most well-established areas of social psychology; no attempt will therefore be made to cover it exhaustively. The strategy of bargaining, in contrast, is still in its infancy as a field of research, and it will therefore be possible to make only a few generalised comments, although it must be stressed that bargaining is at least as important as attitude change for a genuine understanding of the behaviour of pressure groups and related phenomena.

A few scattered studies of attitude change were carried out by social psychologists in the 1920s and 1930s, but it was during World War II that the solid foundations were laid by Carl Hovland in the United States. The problems which motivated his early research were directly pragmatic: how to indoctrinate reluctant army recruits and the general public into believing in the American and Allied cause against Nazi Germany, and how best to combat counter-propaganda. The field soon expanded to embrace wider issues of attitude change and persuasion, and continued after the war at Yale University and subsequently at other research centres in the United States and abroad. The categories of variables examined in the attitude-change process have been conveniently captured by the question: *Who* says *what* to *whom* through what *channel*? These are normally referred to as source, message, audience and channel variables.

Most of the research on source variables has focused on prestige and credibility. The reason why advertisers frequently enlist the costly services of famous personalities to sell their products is that messages delivered by sources of high prestige tend to be more persuasive than those from sources of low prestige. The influence on public opinion of such pressure groups as the Campaign for Nuclear Disarmament owed a great deal to the conspicious support they received from such highly regarded personalities as Bertrand Russell. The connection between prestige and credibility is not of course, a startling discovery, nor is it a new one; Aristotle wrote in his *Rhetoric,* the attitude change manual of its day, that 'we believe good men more fully and readily than others; this is true generally whatever the question is'. The personal quality which makes some people more persuasive than others was referred to by Aristotle as *ethos,* and corresponds to the modern term *credibility.* Research on communicator credibility has, however, revealed some less obvious facts as well. Chief among these is the 'sleeper' effect: when the same message is delivered by a high-credibility source to half the audience and a low-credibility source to the rest, the greater initial impact of the high-credibility source tends to evaporate over a period of a few weeks, but, more surprisingly, the impact of the low-credibility source gradually increases by a sort of delayed action. Both halves of the audience display the same amount of attitude change in the long run, as if they remember only the arguments, not who delivered them.

Further research on the nature of credibility has revealed that the quality which makes some people more persuasive than others is compounded of apparent trustworthiness and expertness which combine multiplicatively rather than additively, so that if either is entirely absent, overall credibility will be zero, since any value multiplied by zero remains zero. The most persuasive spokesman is accordingly someone whom the audience has reason to believe firstly has no ulterior reason for arguing the case in question, and secondly knows what he is talking about. Expertness obviously depends upon the credentials of the source; the views of the Chancellor of the Exchequer on the state of the economy have to be taken seriously, but he may not be believed if he is thought to have good reasons for presenting a biased picture. Convincing the audience of one's trustworthiness is, in fact, a major problem facing anyone engaged in a persuasive appeal. One ingenious method of ensuring trustworthiness which has proved extremely effective in the laboratory, is by allowing the audience to 'overhear' the speaker expressing his viewpoint casually to a friend or colleague, apparently unaware that anyone else is listening. Messages received under these conditions are very much more persuasive than those which appear as calculated attempts at persuasion, since the latter usually raise at least some doubts about trustworthiness and tend to raise defences in the audience.

Message variables have been subjected to close scrutiny by research workers, but the findings have often turned out to be unclear or even contradictory. Numerous experimenters have, for example, attempted to unravel the Gordian knot of data surrounding primacy and recency effects, but the strands now appear more tangled than ever. In 1925, on the basis of only one experiment, and a blatantly flawed one at that, F. H. Lund propounded the so-called Law of Primacy in Persuasion, which asserted that if an audience is exposed to two conflicting arguments on an issue, the argument which is presented first exerts the greater persuasive influence. If this law were valid, it would have the most far-reaching implications, not only for pressure groups and other would-be persuaders of the public at large, but also for parliamentary debates and courtroom proceedings. Careful investigation by Hovland, however, forced him to conclude three decades later that 'when two sides of an issue are present successively by different communicators, the side presented first does not necessarily have the advantage'. Although various complex interactions between primacy, recency and a host of other seemingly related variables have been suggested by more recent work, Hovland's comment remains a fair reflection of our present state of ignorance.

Pressure groups and other agents of attitude change can derive more valuable counsel from the findings on one-sided versus two-sided persuasive communications. The former simply present the communicator's own point of view, while the latter include arguments from the opposing side together with appropriate rebuttals. The most important discovery in this area has been that whereas one-sided messages are, under certain specified conditions, more effective than two-sided messages, two-sided presentations nevertheless induce a greater resistance to counter-propaganda in the audience. A two-sided message sometimes (though by no means always) results in a relatively small initial attitude change, but in any event it has the effect of inoculating the audience against arguments they may later encounter from the opposition, even, curiously enough, when the arguments actually used by the opposition are completely different from those discussed in the original two-sided persuasive message.

An interesting special case involves beliefs which are almost universally accepted by members of a given culture, so that most people have never heard them questioned or even entertained such a possibility. In the early 1960s William McGuire identified several such 'cultural truisms' in the United States. A typical example is: 'It is a good idea to brush your teeth three times a day if possible'. On the basis of a biological analogy, McGuire predicted that these cultural truisms would turn out to be extremely vulnerable to persuasive arguments attacking them. The point is that they have developed in a 'germ-free' environment, never having been subjected to even small doses· of an attacking virus. Organisms which have developed in sterile environments appear superficially to be robust and healthy, as do cultural truisms, but they are in fact unable to resist later exposure to germs. Most controversial beliefs, like most organisms, have over time been repeatedly exposed to varying doses of the attacking arguments or germs, and are therefore more or less resistant to persuasion or disease. McGuire was able to demonstrate that the resistance of cultural truisms to persuasion, which is normally very low, can be greatly increased by inoculation. The method of inoculation, which is based on an extension of the biological analogy, consists of exposing the audience to a few relatively weak arguments against the cultural truism, together with rebuttals, before the massive persuasive onslaught. The process of inoculation is essentially identical to exposing the audience to two-sided persuasive messages in favour of the cultural truisms.

Apart from neglecting to present two-sided messages, which are clearly indicated by the considerations above, individuals and pressure groups frequently water down their persuasive communications out of a fear of alienating their sympathisers and producing the dreaded 'backlash' if they articulate too extreme a position. The National Union of Students, for example, may seriously consider campaigning for a doubling of student grants, but eventually settle on a more modest request in the belief that the milder version has a chance of gaining support, whereas asking for too much may actually lead to a loss of support.

Discrepancy effects, as they are called, have received a considerable amount of attention over the past fifteen years, and it is worth noting that, despite numerous attempts, no experimenter has ever produced a significant negative change by exposing people to too extreme an argument. If not in fact a myth, the backlash phenomenon would therefore seem to be far less ubiquitous than might have been anticipated. When presented by a low-credibility source, an extreme appeal may be less effective than a more moderate one, but it never seems to actually harm the cause, and in virtually all other cases the greatest attitude change results from the most extreme appeal until a limit of absurdity is reached. In one typical experiment, an attempt was made to persuade the subjects that the ideal number of hours of sleep was less than the conventional seven or eight. It was found that a 'Nobel Prize-winning physiologist' produced the greatest change in the subjects' opinions when he advocated one hour of sleep a night, while a source of low credibility was most effective when advocating three hours. Taken as a whole, research findings in this area would seem to suggest that the appropriate strategy for a reasonably credible pressure group spokesman wishing to shift public opinion on some issue, is to articulate his position uncompromisingly, however discrepant it is from that of his audience, rather than to dilute his beliefs for public consumption in the hope of winning more support by appearing more reasonable or moderate. The uncompromising approach is likely to produce the maximum attitude change, and there is nothing in the literature to suggest that he could ever damage his cause by over-selling it, in spite of the received ideas of seasoned political campaigners.

Audience variables have been extremely analysed, but there is no point in treating them in depth here, since they seem to be of only indirect relevance to the problems confronting pressure groups. A very brief résumé would not, however, be out of place.

A rather weak trait of general persuasibility has been established: some people are undoubtedly slightly more persuasible than others, irrespective of the issues (within fairly broad limits) on which they are persuaded. Attempts to link this trait up with specific personality characteristics have led to disappointing results. The level of intelligence of the audience, for example, does not appear to relate to general persuasibility in any consistent way except at the lower extreme: mentally defective individuals may be resistant to persuasion because of their inability to comprehend arguments. The most suggestive findings concern self-esteem; there is some evidence to suggest that people of low self-esteem are more generally persuasible than others. This may be because, having a low opinion of themselves in general, they have a low opinion of their attitudes in particular and therefore give more weight to the attitudes of others, or because they are anxious to improve their self-images by ingratiating themselves with others through agreeing with them, or for a number of other plausible reasons.

Work on channel variables has produced results which are more straightforward and have clearer implications for pressure groups. Repeated studies have shown that identical messages produce markedly different levels of attitude change in audiences depending on the channel through which they are communicated. Most effective by far is face-to-face communication, then in descending order of effectiveness come films, television, radio, and least effective of all, the printed word.

One of the reasons for the relative ineffectiveness of appeals presented through the various mass media may be the phenomenon known as selective exposure. Leaving aside the theoretical background and empirical controversies which would need discussion in a more detailed treatment, selective exposure refers to the tendency of most people actively to seek exposure to arguments which contradict them. People can more easily 'switch off' (literally or metaphorically) an appeal presented through the mass media than one presented face to face. Groups attempting to influence public opinion are usually more successful, therefore, when they supplement their mass media communications with meetings, door-to-door canvassing and other forms of face-to-face persuasion. This seems to have been intuitively appreciated by many religious movements, and undoubtedly accounts, in part, for their propagandistic successes. The same may be said of the People's Liberation Army in China during and after the revolution.

The question of the effectiveness of messages presented through the mass media raises what at first seems to be a paradox. On the one hand, as every politician and advertiser knows, persuasive appeals in the media often result in significant changes in public opinion, but on the other, it has been firmly established that the overwhelming majority of people are not persuaded to any noticeable extent by mere exposure to such messages; when their attitudes do change, the effect can usually be traced to face-to-face encounters of some kind or other. This apparent contradiction was a source of embarrassment to social psychologists for many years, until it was resolved in the late 1940s by Paul Lazarsfeld's discovery of the two-step flow of information. In the course of a detailed panel study of a Presidential election, which involved the repeated interviewing of a representative sample throughout the campaign, Lazarsfeld and his co-workers found that mass media appeals did indeed produce significant shifts in public opinion, but that this effect was for the most part indirect. A small minority of people in all sections of the community, whom they labelled opinion leaders, were directly persuaded by the mass media appeals, and they in turn influenced large numbers of friends, relatives and acquaintances through face-to-face encounters, thereby setting off a sort of chain reaction among the rank and file. Thus most people were more or less unmoved by direct exposure to mass communications, but the effects ultimately reached them indirectly, by way of the two-step flow of information. This mechanism has been shown to operate in the dissemination of new ideas from the spread of clothing fashions among women to the adoption of new drugs by general practitioners. It should be recognised, therefore, that the immediate target of a mass media appeal is not the public at large, but a tiny army of opinion leaders. A failure to appreciate this fact frequently results in condescending messages which insult the intelligence, background knowledge and attentiveness of these key members of the audience.

Successful attempts by pressure groups to change government policy by mere persuasion, either directly or through mobilisation of mass support, are comparatively rare, and each positive instance in Britain (such as the suffragette movement in the early 1900s or the Commercial Television lobby in the 1950s) can be countered by numerous unsuccessful campaigns (the Campaign for Nuclear Disarmament, the Stop The Seventy Tour Campaign, the Biafra Lobby and so on). Pressure groups which command the necessary resources to engage the government in genuine bargaining are, on the other hand, much better placed to influence decisions, and not infrequently achieve their goals relatively quickly and easily. It is therefore necessary, for the sake of completeness, to discuss briefly some of the scattered results which have been reached through strategic analyses of bargaining situations by informal game theorists. Most pertinent is the pioneering work of Thomas C. Schelling, from whose book *The Strategy of Conflict* (Oxford, 1963) the discussion will draw heavily.

A pressure group finds itself in a bargaining situation *vis-à-vis* the government when the ability of each to achieve certain desired ends depends upon what the other does. The National Union of Mineworkers may, for example, desire a pay rise for its members which would exceed a government's limit on wage increases and breach its anti-inflationary policy. Or the Provisional IRA may wish the government to transfer convicted bomb planters from prisons in England to Northern Ireland. Or finally, the British Medical Association may seek to resist a proposed government policy of forbidding its members to use National Health facilities and hospital beds for treating private patients. In each case a genuine bargaining situation exists because of the mutual inter-dependence of the decisions which each side can make. Each of these pressure groups depends upon government action to achieve its goal, and the government, for its part, depends upon the mineworkers not going on strike, the Provisionals not escalating their bombing campaign, and the doctors not withdrawing from the National Health Service or even emigrating.

The most striking conclusion which has emerged from a theoretical analysis of such situations is somewhat counter-intuitive; it contradicts conventional wisdom and 'common sense'. It is that bargaining power derives largely from some voluntary and irreversible sacrifice of freedom of choice. 'Keeping all options open' is a faulty policy based on incomplete understanding, and one which may significantly weaken one's bargaining position. The practice among invading armies of burning their bridges (or boats) and thereby voluntarily relinquishing the option of withdrawing, is strategically analogous to the tactic of the suffragettes of chaining themselves to the railings. By this action they rendered themselves impervious to threats to disperse or be punished. The National Union of Mineworkers, in the example cited above, would greatly increase its bargaining power at the conference table if it could demonstrate that it was simply not able to accept a wage settlement below a certain level, since its members had *already* voted to go on strike unless the settlement exceeded this limit. In practice, trade unions normally delay such votes until their negotiators have provisionally accepted an offer, in the belief that tying the hands of the negotiators would sap their bargaining strength. Flexible negotiators with full authority from their members to accept any offer at their own discretion are, on the contrary, the relatively weak ones.

The analysis of threats has led to similar conclusions. It is of the essence of a threat that neither the threatening party nor the recipient wishes it to be carried out. A threat by the mineworkers to call a strike unless their pay demands are met would clearly display this property; neither the mineworkers nor the government desires a strike. So would a threat by doctors to withdraw from the National Health Service unless their wishes are granted. And a threat by the Provisionals to blow up Westminster unless certain prisoners are transferred to Northern Ireland may be something they would far rather not have to carry out. A major problem which the protagonist always has to solve, therefore, is how to make his threat credible. Here again, the solution often lies in voluntarily relinquishing freedom of action. A sniper on the rampage in a public street would be invulnerable to arrest if he was known to be wired up with dynamite in such a way that any attempt to arrest him would result in an explosion killing himself and everyone within a half-mile radius. If, however, he had some visible means of preventing the detonation, the police might be more likely to risk an arrest, since the threat to kill himself (and others) would be much less credible and could be interpreted as a bluff. A related tactic often used by pressure groups (and governments) to make their threats credible is the establishment of precedents. The Provisionals' threat might be believed because they have done such things in the past, but a bomb threat from the British Medical Association would be treated as a joke in poor taste.

A counter-tactic in the face of an imminent threat is to interfere with the channels of communication. Most parents, and apparently some of their children, realise that an injunction to 'stop crying' together with a threat 'or you'll get no ice-cream' is ineffective if it cannot be heard above the din. Schelling has suggested that a law requiring all interested friends and relatives of a kidnap victim to be held incommunicado in prison, thus making it impossible for the kidnapper to communicate his threats, would make the prospects for exacting ransom seem unprofitably dim, and it is worth adding that such a law would probably never have to be enforced in practice. Similarly, if the government could convince the Provisionals that so many hoax threats are received every day that it is impossible to identify the genuine ones, the power of the Provisionals to issue effective threats would be placed in jeopardy. A secret code-word, known only to the Provisionals and the authorities is, in fact, presently used in communications for this very reason, but circumstances could arise in which it would be in the government's interest to leak the code-word to the press, thereby disrupting the communication system. An ultra-subtle manoeuvre on the part of the Provisionals would be to pre-empt a government press leak by themselves 'leaking' a variety of false code-words. These fanciful suggestions merely go to show that the strategic connection between the availability of threats and the possibility of transmitting unambiguous messages is a complex one. Enough has been said, however, to discredit the widely-held dogma that, in bargaining situations, it is always to one's advantage to keep the lines of communication open.

It follows from the above analysis that, in some circumstances, communication with the opposition can positively harm the interests of one of the protagonists in a dispute. Experienced negotiators never seem to tire of reassuring their followers that it is always a good idea to meet the opposition over the conference table, and that talking with the adversary cannot possibly do any harm, but these assertions can easily be refuted with the aid of a hypothetical example. Suppose that the government were committed to granting an amnesty to twenty of the prisoners being held in Northern Ireland gaols, and proposed a secret conference with the Provisionals to help draw up a list of suitable candidates. Were the Provisionals to attend such a conference, they might be subjected to the threat that unless they stopped their bombing campaign, none of their members would be included in the amnesty. Assuming further that, had the meeting not taken place, the government would have had no incentive to exclude Provisional members from the amnesty, it is not difficult to see that merely by making themselves available for negotiation at the conference table, the Provisionals would have significantly damaged their own interests.

A poignant example of this bargaining paradox occurs in Act II of Shakespeare's *Measure for Measure*. Angelo is holding a prisoner whom he intends to execute. The prisoner's sister, Isabella, who is apparently not well-versed in informal game theory, arrives to plead for her brother's life. Angelo is strongly attracted to Isabella and at length he proposes a dishonourable bargain—'You must lay down the treasures of your body'—in order to save him. Isabella declines the offer—'More than our brother is our chastity'—whereupon Angelo threatens not merely to kill the prisoner, as he had originally intended, but to subject him to a lingering death unless she submits. At this point Isabella finds herself in a worse position than before the meeting, out of which she has clearly derived only negative value, and if Angelo's threat is to be believed, her brother is also worse off.

Certain important strategic properties inhere in bargaining situations which force a protagonist to expose himself to risk in order to threaten his adversary, so that, although the threat may be issued unilaterally, punishment is always bilateral if it is carried out. Such situations are known technically as dangerous games. A typical example, which depends on the existence of certain structural features which cannot be explained here, is the game of 'chicken'. 'Chicken' may be played by teenagers, who have been known to drive cars towards each other in an open field as a test of nerves; the winner is the one who holds out the longer before swerving out of the collision course. It may, however, also be played by two superpowers in an arms race, or, in certain circumstances, by the Trade Union Congress and the government.

A curious and once again somewhat paradoxical feature of such games is the advantage which goes to a protagonist who behaves irrationally. If one of the players in a game of automobile 'chicken' could convince the opponent that he had lost control of his rational facilities, by drinking half a bottle of whisky before the game for example, he would greatly increase his chances of winning against a rational opponent. If both players adopted this strategy, however, a catastrophic outcome would be likely. What Daniel Ellsberg has called 'the political uses of madness' would arise similarly if the Trades Union Congress threatened to call an extended general strike unless some piece of industrial legislation were repealed. If the leaders were able to convince the government that they were entirely at the mercy of a hysterical mob which could not be reasoned with, their bargaining power would be greatly increased. On the other hand, if the piece of legislation at stake were comparatively trivial, it would be difficult for the government to prove in advance that it was so unreasonable that it would rather face an extended general strike than make a small concession, whether this was true or not.

The process of bargaining and persuasive attitude change are not, of course, mutually exclusive. The Mineworkers' Union, the Provisional IRA and the British Medical Association may all engage in attempts to persuade the government and the general public of the justice of their demands while at the same time exerting influence through strategic bargaining manoeuvres. Pressure groups which do not command the necessary resources to bargain directly, which is the case with most promotional or cause groups, are, on the other hand, bound to restrict their efforts to attempts at persuasion. Mary Whitehouse's National Viewers and Listeners Association and the Anti-Apartheid Movement, to mention two typical cases, may depend upon government action to achieve their ends, but they cannot bargain, because the government does not depend upon them in any concrete sense. The success of their campaigns therefore rests solely on the effectiveness of their persuasive appeals. The fairly impressive literature on the psychology of attitude change and the suggestive theoretical analysis of the strategy of bargaining which have been outlined above go some way towards a proper understanding of the activities of pressure groups. Perhaps the most important conclusion which can be drawn from this discussion is that the conventional wisdom which guides these activities may not always be adequate to the problems in hand or generate the most effective policies.

# THE AID LOBBY          JUDITH YOUNG

A combination of factors makes the aid lobby unusual among interest groups. It is a promotional lobby, yet not for the interests of its members but for ideals that are based on self denial rather than self interest. It is concerned with Britain's policies overseas, and yet at the same time it aims to change the pattern of government spending at home. Its membership is small, and yet it has accepted that to achieve its aims the beliefs and prejudices of a good proportion of the British electorate must be changed.

Overseas aid has always tended to fall between departmental stools. Before 1964, seven departments were concerned in one way or another with its administration, and even the creation of the independent Ministry of Overseas Development (ODM) by the newly elected Labour Government in October 1964 failed to solve the problem entirely. There is always a tendency for a government to want to use overseas aid as part of its foreign policy: to punish Tanzania for hostility over Rhodesia or to compensate the Maltese for British withdrawals. But at the same time, the sending of large sums of money overseas involves the Treasury—a department which during the years of the Labour Government was concerned above all else with the balance of payments problem and 'stretching' resources to finance rapidly growing government expenditure. A third factor is the Cabinet, which resolves interdepartmental disputes and outlines general policies. Ministers as individuals may be sympathetic to causes such as overseas aid, but the very structure of the Cabinet means that they are concerned primarily with defending or extending the spending power of their own departments.

Most lobbies have as their first aim the ministry dealing with their particular area: they aim to set up a close working relationship with the ministry and to persuade ministers and civil servants to adopt their plans or to amend existing policies in their favour. This is all very well when the ministry is strong with a Cabinet minister at its head, but in the case of a weak, non-Cabinet ministry—which was the position of the ODM from January 1967—there is little point in a lobby convincing a ministry that something must be done when the weakness of that ministry means that the stronger ministries and the Treasury are likely to overrule any change in policy. As a result of this, many of those concerned about overseas aid realised that there was little point in concentrating their fire on the ODM, since those they met in lobbying were as concerned and committed as they themselves and yet even more powerless to take effective action.

Before considering the ways in which the aid lobby has organised itself and has taken political action, it is necessary to look a little more closely at its component parts. To those involved in the lobby, generalisations about the lobby as a whole must lack validity, and some lobbyists will consider that their aims and methods are totally different from those of their fellows. This is a factor typical of many lobbies, however, and generalisation is unavoidable if the movement as a whole is to be examined. In this context, it is perhaps best to look at the particular and then broaden to the general.

Two basic lines of definition exist in the aid lobby. First there is the vertical axis travelling from central co-ordinating bodies down to local activists, and secondly there is a horizontal political spectrum stretching from right wing conservation to left wing radicalism. The bodies described below fall as points close to one or both of these axes, and consideration of them as such will perhaps provide a useful framework by which a study of the movement may be structured.

Close to the first axis can be found the central co-ordinating bodies. The earliest of these was probably the Freedom From Hunger Campaign (FFHC) which united other overseas charities in the 1960–65 campaign against world hunger. FFHC is now, however, a charity in its own right. Its place was taken in late 1965 by the Voluntary Committee on Overseas Aid and Development (VCOAD), a body set up by the Catholic Institute for International Relations, Christian Aid, FFHC, Overseas Development Institute (ODI), Oxfam, Save the Children Fund, United Nations Association (UNA), and War on Want 'to coordinate their efforts in the fields of education in British schools and colleges, public information and overseas projects. It is the medium through which organisations interested in aid and development can represent their views to the Government' *(Vox)*.

VCOAD has had three main achievements in the political and educational field: the first has been the production of *Vox*, a monthly magazine giving development news, details of current campaigns, and reviews of new publications in the field of overseas development. This has proved to be a well-produced periodical, and has done a great deal to establish links between aid lobbyists throughout the country. It is also read by a number of influential MPs. The second was the founding of the first local groups of aid lobbyists—often called World Poverty Action Groups (WPAGs)—from 1967 onwards, and the third was the development of close personal contacts between members of VCOAD and the ODM which blossomed into a close working relationship. VCOAD became fully accepted as a responsible and respected body by the ministry and benefitted accordingly.

Sharing the same London building as VCOAD is Action for World Development (AWD). This was set up in 1969 by the same bodies that set up VCOAD, with the exception of the Save the Children Fund and the Freedom From Hunger Campaign , both of which declined to join so overtly political a body. The manifesto issued by AWD and its setting up stated the aims of the charities concerned:

> We shall raise money for development projects; we shall keep the problems of the developing countries constantly before the attention of the British people, and we shall stimulate the political will which is the essential prerequisite of government action.
>
> The division of mankind into rich and poor is the greatest problem of our time. It will not be solved by those who have the power to solve it—the governments of the rich nations—unless individuals who believe that it must be solved make their voices heard. We therefore invite individuals and groups in Britain to join us in the struggle for world development.

The Charity Commissioners who closely watch any political moves taken by charities were unhappy at the attitude taken by AWD; as a result, it became the AWD Trust in May 1970, financed by the Rowntree Trust rather than the charities, and thus more independent of its founder members.

The main success of AWD has been not so much in actions taken by the central body (AWD found penetration of the mass media almost impossible during the 1970 election), but in its encouragement and co-ordination of local WPAGs, a function it took over from VCOAD. The importance of these local groups to the aid movement as a whole cannot be over-emphasised.

Local groups have become the instruments for and the instigators of two kinds of lobbying. The first, and more difficult, is public education. By setting up displays at public functions, asking people to sign petitions, publishing pamphlets, holding conferences, talking to local societies, and holding demonstrations, a good local group can do a great deal to make a normally apathetic public aware of the problems of world poverty and what can be done about it. The second type of lobbying consists of exerting pressure on local MPs. When a group is well known in a locality, an MP will find it hard to resist meeting its members either at the Commons or at local gatherings. If the MP is in favour of more and better government aid then he will greatly value the support of such a group in what is normally not too popular a stand; if he opposes increased aid or wants to impose stringent conditions on it, then he will have to produce logical and informed arguments in support of his case and may well be inclined to modify his views. Some of the more successful local groups such as the Kensington and Chelsea and Sheffield WPAGs have exerted a considerable influence in this way.

Although local groups can achieve success on their own, it has been their co-ordination by AWD which has given them real strength. It has meant that when information about possible aid cuts or new government policies has reached the London office, local groups can be contacted quickly and easily and their support mobilised as required. In addition, local groups have been able to obtain ideas and educational material easily and cheaply through VCOAD and AWD. This country-wide co-ordination is perhaps the most important lesson that the aid lobby can teach other bodies: it has accounted for the chief successes of the movement to date.

At the 'right' of the horizontal or political axis are bodies such as the Save the Children Fund and the Freedom From Hunger Campaign, which prefer to leave the main part of their educational work to VCOAD and to concentrate upon fund raising. Those running these charities tend to be pragmatic and to strive for an obtainable financial target rather than pressing for an overall solution which would involve more government aid. In contrast, most of the other overseas charities tend to look with more favour on political action as being essential if their own work is not to be meaningless. War on Want has stressed the need for more government aid ever since the 1950s and has always encouraged its members to write to MPs and Ministers on such matters. Oxfam also did a great deal in the early 1960s to increase public awareness about overseas development through advertising campaigns and well-produced educational material. Christian Aid was especially important from 1966 onwards in encouraging Christians to be informed about development problems and, more importantly, involved in trying to solve them. *World Poverty and British Responsibility,* an informative pamphlet written by a panel of experts and published in 1966 by the British Council of Churches, called not only for increased private charity but also for more public pressure for better government aid: 'Finally, since governments will only do what public opinion will support or demand, individuals can help by studying these problems and promoting discussion of them in their churches, in study groups, political activity and in conversation with their friends' (P62). It was such activity that led to many Christians becoming involved in the overseas development movement and to the formation of the first local groups. The majority of those involved in the aid lobby were and are active Christians, and the action of the British Council of Churches and Christian Aid must have been instrumental in this.

It might be asked why the charities should have become involved at all in lobbying for more overseas aid. The fact is that they became aware, in turn, of how little was their contribution in contrast with the funds available to the government. In 1967, for example, the aid organisations, by dint of much hard effort, collected a total of about £8 millions. For the same year, however, government aid totals were cut by £20 millions. This alone made many charity workers realise that their work was achieving little if the government could slash aid totals by two and a half times all that their efforts had collected, and thus many became drawn into political action.

Apart from the charities, there are three important educational groups which have participated in the lobby. The first of these is the Overseas Development Institute, a body financed by private industry, which studies in depth problems of development and produces informed pamphlets and speakers on the subject. The views of the ODI are treated with considerable respect by both governments and academics, and its members have considerable personal influence with those in influential positions. The United Nations Association is primarily concerned with educating the public about the UN, but since the main preoccupation of that body since 1960 has been world development, UNA has lobbied both individually and with other members of VCOAD and AWD for improved British Government aid. Of special importance has been the all-party UN Parliamentary Committee within the House of Commons, which has heard many speakers on overseas development, accepted UN briefs and asked parliamentary questions as a result. Many of the demands of the aid lobby—that overseas aid should be one per cent of the Gross National Product, that trade conditions should be made to favour the poor world, and so forth—originated with UNA, which did much to promote Paul Hoffman's *A Hundred Countries, One and a Quarter Billion People* (Committee for International Growth, Washington, 1960) which first gave these ideas a serious economical base. The third educational body of great importance has been the Catholic Institute for International Relations, an educational charity which has narrowed its field of interest since 1966 to concentrate increasingly on the problems of the developing world. It works closely with the Commission for Justice and Peace, set up to advise the Catholic hierarchy on the Church's responsibilities in the world, and these two bodies have done a great deal to educate Catholics of the importance of giving aid to the developing world.

To the 'left' of the aid movement are the youth groups, of which three are particularly worthy of mention. The first and most famous is the Haslemere Group, formed in 1968 to 'discuss the social and economic crisis facing the "developing countries" of Afro-Asia and Latin America, the failure of the rich industrialised countries such as Britain to recognise their responsibility for this crisis and the urgent need to draw effective public attention to these issues' (The Haslemere Declaration, P1). The Haslemere Declaration was signed, calling for a programme of true world development rather than charitable giving by rich to poor, and for the creation of a new economic and social order in the world in a spirit of tolerance and humanity. As a result, campaigns have been mounted to support liberation movements and to oppose economic exploitation, but the deliberately loose organisation of the group—which expanded rapidly from the original forty signatories—has tended to decrease its effectiveness.

Somewhat similar views are expressed by VCOAD's Youth and Universities Unit, which has acted as a co-ordinating unit for young people and has also produced a well-written and radical newsletter discussing development issues. Both the Haslemere Group and the Youth and Universities Unit have done much to mobilise young people to think, argue, and demonstrate against world poverty; the problem they have encountered is that the enemy seems too enormous, for it includes in their view the world economic order of the present, dominated by selfish rich countries and also many of the repressive governments of the poor nations. It is difficult to sustain the battle against such a mass of powerful and ill-defined forces, and the effort can lead to despair and disillusion.

One group of young people which avoided this problem to some extent by limiting its aims to the politically possible was the New Abolitionists, now split among the other bodies mentioned above. The group took its name from a phrase used by Barbara Ward (Lady Jackson) in 1967 when she referred to the long-term campaign of the Abolitionists who fought in and through Parliament to abolish slavery: 'We need the new Abolitionists who say that our small planet cannot survive half wealthy beyond all dreams and half in poverty-stricken starvation'.

The New Abolitionists discussed the problem of overseas development and decided to try to change the policy of the British Government through the parliamentary machinery. Each member wrote to MPs and met them at the House of Commons if possible. Their approach was careful and informed, as Raymond Fletcher MP wrote in the *Guardian*: 'They have grasped an essential and almost wholly obscured truth about the temporary residents in the Palace of Westminster. There are very few complete heels among us. Successful political villainy requires hard work and many of those who have the ambition to do a Machiavelli lack the stamina. Good nature keeps breaking in and dilutes the demon's drive. Nearly all of us are desperately anxious to do the right thing' (21 October 1968).

The New Abolitionists built up contacts with sympathetic MPs and were able to brief them with material for Parliamentary Questions and for debates. In addition, they also pressed MPs to ask for a Select Committee on Overseas Aid to be set up so that the whole subject would be given wide publicity and the government would feel the need to listen to the views of MPs. This aim was achieved and the Committee was set up, although not by the New Abolitionists alone.

There were and are other groups that could be mentioned, and it is space rather than a denial of their importance that prevents their names appearing. What has been said already about the differing aims and methods of the groups described should show that to talk about the 'aid lobby' is a rather inaccurate generalisation. Some of these bodies concerned with economic development on both 'right' and 'left' reject political action as being less desirable than charity or revolution respectively. The rest of this article concentrates on those in the 'centre' who accept political action and looks more closely at the methods they use.

Action aimed at improving British aid has concentrated on two main fronts: educating public opinion and influencing government policy. Although both of these present difficulties, the first is obviously a much more ambitious goal, and yet lobbyists are aware that they need the support of a reasonably large section of the public before they can persuade any government to make large increases in the aid programme.

The public can be split roughly into two halves: there are people aware of the problems of overseas development who need to be prodded to give money or take some form of direct political action, and there are the vast masses of people who are apathetic or even hostile to sending money abroad to help others or who will not accept that the terms of international trade should be altered to favour Britain less and the poor world more.

There is a tendency for people to be able to ignore what is far away and out of sight. If a child lay starving in the gutters of Dulwich, there can be little doubt that passers-by would rush to help and would be appalled by the fact such a thing could happen, and yet public opinion polls indicate that overseas aid is one of the first things that people wish to see cut whenever there is an economic crisis. It is pointless sending information sheets to such people; the problem has to be tackled in a more urgent and shocking manner. Christian Aid, for example, tries to do this in its advertisements. In December 1969, the story of the Nativity was presented with a new emphasis, beneath a reproduction of Poussin's *The Adoration of the Shepherds*:

How much longer are we going to put up with all this ? The Year of Our Lord 1969. And babies are still being born in Middle East stables.
On rubbish tips in South America.
In shanties all over Asia.
Some progress we've made since Christ in His love for man was born into poverty.
Yet the politicians consistently do less about it.
This May, the richest country in history pushed through its lowest foreign aid budget in twenty years. While Britain parts with £1 million less than she did nine years ago.
The unhappy outcome of this is that Christian Aid is needed more than ever.
Not just to provide more hygienic birthplaces.
But to pay for such luxuries as well drills for drought stricken India.
For teachers for Bolivia, Senegal and Ethiopia. For family planning clinics in Brazil and Ghana.

To fill this need, we ask two things:
Your signature to a 'Sign-In' organised by all the churches for more government aid in the future.
But first of all, your money. For more Christian Aid now.
After all, what use is government aid to a man who starves before it comes?

(*Sunday Times,* 7 December 1969)

The effect of such advertisements may be hard to judge. However, the success of this particular series is perhaps vouched by the fact that the churches' 'Sign-In' mentioned in the advertisement attracted one million signatures with all the resultant publicity.

The second stage of education is to go beyond pity and to seek to inform as many people as possible about the magnitude of development problems. All organisations concerned with overseas development have produced large quantities of good quality literature and even films for schools and for general use. VCOAD has led a quiet campaign to increase the awareness of teachers in the hope that the need for world development will be emphasised to children in geography and economics lessons.

A different approach has been to stress self-interest with catch-phrases such as 'Overseas aid helps British trade' and information concerning the vast potential markets that aid could open up. Another similar theme is the danger in which the children of the present generation could find themselves if two thirds of the world is still starving while world resources are allowed to grow scarcer and population figures soar.

It is hard to assess how successful such campaigns have been. One indication of success may be the fact that the demand for information from aid organisations has steadily grown greater, so presumably more people are being made aware of development problems. On the other hand, overseas charities are finding that people are more apathetic and less willing to give money: the idealism shown in the early 1960s and inspired by the Freedom From Hunger Campaign seems to have been daunted by a problem that increases rather than diminishes and which is increasingly unknown on a personal level to the majority of Britons. However, the policy of the aid lobby on education is long-term—it cannot be properly assessed until the generation now at school become electors, or perhaps even later than that.

The influence of the aid lobby on the British Government can be seen more clearly and successes and failures are much more marked. The position of the Ministry of Overseas Development has already been mentioned, but its attitude *vis-à-vis* the aid lobby as a whole is most important, and its abolition as an independent body has probably been a considerable setback for the lobby.

Although many of the officials at the Ministry were career civil servants, many of the specialists were not, and their loyalty lay more with the crusade for economic development than with government policy. Consequently, there was a very close liaison between some officials in the Ministry and members of the aid lobby. This relationship also existed between the lobbyists and successive Ministers—Barbara Castle, Anthony Greenwood, Arthur Bottomley, Reg Prentice, Judith Hart and Richard Wood. It is therefore not surprising to find that in 1965 Sir Andrew Cohen, the Permanent Secretary at the ODM, did much to encourage the overseas agencies to co-ordinate their efforts in the body that was to be VCOAD, thus creating a body which had as one of its professed aims lobbying the government for more and better aid. Then in 1969, when news of impending cuts reached the aid lobbyists, it had been leaked by ministry officials with the tacit approval of the Minister. The very nature of overseas development tended to fill successive Ministers with crusading fervour and to change their loyalties in some cases to international rather than national policies. The Prime Minister grew concerned about this in the case of Reg Prentice and in the autumn of 1969 he moved him to the Ministry of Technology. Prentice resigned a few days later, saying in his letter of resignation: 'I would prefer to work for things I consider as very important as a backbencher and in the country without having ministerial duties which would have prevented me from speaking out on other issues.' He later added, 'I was the fourth of the Labour Ministers of Overseas Development. All of us have had to fight some tough battles within the Government and we have by no means lost them all. But the record shows that we have not been able to persuade our colleagues to give a high priority of aid' (*New Statesman*, 17 October 1969). It was not only Labour Ministers who reacted strongly to this conflict of loyalties, if this quotation from the *Observer* of 12 July 1970 was correct. It refers to the campaign to preserve the ODM as an independent ministry:

'The MOD (ODM) has attracted an admirable group of civil servants, men with an almost missionary zeal. They are not above bending the ears of journalists and MPs—Tories especially—to argue the case for an independent Ministry. Nor is Richard Wood (son of the late Lord Halifax) too upset by his staff's extra-curricular activities. He's not above bending some ears himself.'

It was this type of dedication to overseas development that made lobbying the ODM rather pointless. However, token lobbies were made so that favourable figures indicating public concern could be given as answers to parliamentary questions. In 1969, the Ministry received about 1500 letters calling for more and better aid—many of them as part of a planned lobby—while only 25 were received opposing increased aid. In addition, groups of those concerned regularly visited the Minister or one of his high officials to present their views or proposals for policy changes.

On the whole, the ODM and the aid lobby were fairly independent from the time that the Ministry lost its Cabinet seat until the abolition of the ODM. The aid lobby needed to have a close relationship with the Ministry in order to gain information and to influence details of policy. The Ministry needed the lobby as a safety net so that when a battle with the Cabinet or Treasury was lost, the lobby could mount a public campaign to prevent cuts in aid totals or changes in allocations. This policy was publicly stated in a ministerial reply to a criticism made by the Select Committee on Overseas Aid that 'special consideration should be given to making the aid problem more familiar to the public at large in a form which they can readily understand'. Richard Wood replied that 'The Minister accepts the need for a better informed public opinion, but believes it right to concentrate most available resources on informing those groups and individuals who are in turn conducting extensive publicity and educational campaigns'. The ODM was thus prepared to make full use of bodies seemingly independent of it in its own defence. Since the ODM was a weak ministry in a government which had a rapidly expanding programme of spending, it could not hope to compete with giants in the Cabinet such as Defence and Education. Anthony Crossland, who as Secretary of State for Education was one of those giants, wrote describing how difficult such battles were even for his powerful ministry. In answer to the question 'How does a Minister get enough resources for his service?' he said, 'By persuading, arguing, cajoling, exploiting his political position, being a bloody nuisance in the Cabinet. Above all by being persistent ... It's an endless tactical battle which requires determination, cunning, and occasional unscrupulousness'

(*Sunday Times,* 26 September 1971). If this was the way a powerful minister had to struggle through the difficult period 1966–69, it can be imagined how nearly impossible the same struggle was for a small non-Cabinet ministry sending money abroad in a period of continual currency crises. On the other hand, Harold Wilson in particular and the Cabinet in general had made strong moral commitments about overseas aid before coming into office, and although the Minister of Overseas Development was limited in being able to jog memories, members of the lobby did all that they could to pluck the moral heart-strings of the Government through the House of Commons and direct lobbying.

The power of the House of Commons is generally held today to be in decline, and yet it was through mobilising support in the Commons that the chief direct political success of the lobby was achieved. It was chiefly the result of the slow building up of links between lobbyists and MPs such as those forged by the New Abolitionists, and of the well-maintained lines of communication to groups in constituencies throughout the country.

In May 1969, news was leaked from the ODM of the likelihood of a cut in the aid totals for the next year. Through VCOAD, all the local groups and interested bodies were notified quickly and efficiently, and on 21 July 350 lobbyists descended on the House of Commons and lobbied their MPs. The following day, a Commons early-day motion was put up by the Government not to cut overseas aid, and was signed by nearly 100 MPs almost at once. In addition, the Chancellor of the Exchequer had to admit in Parliament that he had received a thousand letters, while the ODM received 600 and MPs a great number. It was the opinion of the then Minister, Reg Prentice, that it was this well-organised operation that saved the aid total from being cut—he gave full credit to the lobbyists.

In October 1969, Ian Aitken of the *Guardian* sounded a fresh alarm from the Labour Party Conference: 'Backbench MPs attending the Labour Party Conference this week are convinced that the current Cabinet survey of Government expenditure covering the next five years is likely to result in a cut-back in the scale of the overseas aid programme in real terms'. Once again, but this time by means of Action for World Development, the local groups were circularised and a hugh letter-writing campaign was launched, greatly aided by the publicity surrounding Prentice's resignation at this time. When the future aid programme was finally announced after considerable delay the totals were not as high as the lobbyists had wished, but they were considerably better than the limits given by the Treasury to Prentice before his resignation. Frank Judd MP, a leading supporter of overseas development, told some friends in the lobby: 'Do not be disheartened. By your action you have almost certainly prevented an even worse set of figures' (*Vox*, December 1969).

On other occasions, the lobbyists were far less successful. The most noticeable failure was the lack of impact they made during the 1970 election campaign. The announcement of the election took the lobby by surprise, and when the main issues of the election became inflation and the rising cost of living, any group calling for increased funds for overseas development was a voice crying in the wilderness. Lobbyists attended the daily press conferences of the two major parties. At one of these, Reginald Maudling was asked to talk about aid; he replied that the election was not being fought on that issue. When Harold Wilson was asked what had happened to the War on Want (he coined the phrase) he replied: 'I made a statement about that recently' and walked on (*Vox*, June 1970). A flood of material sent to newspapers and magazines on the need to help the developing world was almost completely ignored. This example shows clearly how any lobby like this is dependent on the concern and good will of politicians and the mass media as regards any centrally organised campaign; much more successful were some of the efforts of local groups in individual constituencies, where the attention of politicians and reporters was more easily attracted.

It is too early as yet to assess the movement for overseas development as a whole, considering the shortness of its existence as a political force and the fact that many of its aims are long term. Some attempt has been made throughout this article to point out its most interesting features and to offer some thoughts on strengths and weaknesses. In a sense, the aid lobby is peculiar in that it is involved with the government's foreign as well as financial policies, and it has had some success in influencing politicians in these fields and in Parliament. On the other hand, the organisation and methods of the lobby are a good guide to other similar action groups lacking resources but seeking maximum involvement in the political process. The chief problem it will have to face is maintaining the enthusiasm of its members in the face of frustration: if it can survive the next few years, the aid movement may prove to be the advent of a new style of open lobbying and an important political force in British politics.

# HOMOSEXUAL LAW REFORM

To secure a change in the law relating to sexual behaviour is a task fraught with peculiar difficulties. Nevertheless, in the Parliament of 1966, not one but several such changes were enacted—notably those relating to divorce, abortion and homosexuality. Having been closely concerned with the latter reform during the whole of the ten-year interval between the publication of the Wolfenden Report in 1957 and the passage into law of the 1967 Sexual Offences Act which embodied its main recommendations, I am perhaps well placed to assess the role (and limitations) of pressure groups operating in the more delicate and emotion-charged areas of social change. As Secretary of the Homosexual Law Reform Society (1962–70) I saw democracy at work at close quarters. It was a strenuous and some-times disconcerting experience; and if I had known at the beginning all that was to be entailed, I might have thought twice before taking it on.

For where sex is concerned, one is up against not merely the ordinary prejudice and misinformation which surrounds any political topic: there is an altogether deeper dimension of emotionally-held attitudes which impel those on each side to espouse their causes with a high degree of self-righteousness and consign their opponents to the devil. (I think this was especially true over abortion and homosexuality. We received surprisingly few abusive letters at the HLRS, and most of those which did arrive were anonymous, the writers apparently being apprehensive as to the wisdom of giving their names and addresses lest some awful fate should befall them.) The campaigners for liberalising reforms regard themselves as crusading to end inhumanity and injustice; their opponents look upon them as contributing to the moral downfall of society and 'opening the floodgates' to rampart licentiousness.

How was it, then, that between 1966 and 1969 so many sensitive social issues were tackled by Parliament? Partly, I think, because there were an unusually large number of liberally (small 'l') minded MPs of all parties in that Parliament; but also because the changes they enacted reflected a majority view in the country that the time was ripe for reform in these matters. The Labour Government reacted to the climate of opinion by providing sufficient Parliamentary time for several important private members' Bills to become law on a non-party, free-voting basis.

Pressure groups such as ALRA (the Abortion Law Reform Association) and HLRS undoubtedly played a significant role in this result. How significant? Here I am treading upon delicate ground, having recently incurred the 1967 Sexual Offences Act's Parliamentary sponsors' displeasure by inadvertently remarking on television that 'it took me nearly ten years' hard work to get the law changed', when I should of course have said 'us'. But while I would (needless to say) be very far from claiming that 'alone I (or HLRS, or ALRA) did it', I must risk further displeasure by asserting that without the hard and persistent work of HLRS and ALRA over a period of years before homosexuality and abortion became live Parliamentary issues, the Sexual Offences and Abortion Acts would almost certainly not yet be on the Statute Book.

From the plains, a mountain peak looks distant but startlingly simple and dominant. When you stand upon it, you may find yourself merely on the brink of a range of foothills with much more challenging and arduous goals still ahead. The social reforms of the 1960s may be viewed in this way. Mostly, they embodied recommendations made several years (usually at least a decade) previously which had in the intervening time been the subject of fierce controversy. By the time they were enacted they were all, in some respects, irrelevant to some pressing contemporary needs—yet in the eyes of many of the protagonists, they represented a 'solution' to the problems with which they were concerned. To deny that this was in fact so is in no way to belittle their significance or to underrate the signal achievement of those who succeeded in manoeuvring them through the cumbrous Parliamentary machine.

The results, however, do underline one feature of the role of pressure groups which those seeking to emulate them would do well to face at the outset. This is that, while a pressure group can be, and frequently is, instrumental in achieving its broad objective, it usually has far less influence over the details—or even the general scope—of the legislation in which it is interested than may be thought. This can perhaps best be explained by reviewing the campaign for homosexual law reform historically, as it passed through several successive stages.

First, the pressure group's formation. In our case, this came about some six months after publication of the Wolfenden Committee's report (*Report of the Committee on Homosexual Offences and Prostitution*, Cmnd. 247, September 1957) whose principal recommendation was 'that homosexual behaviour between consenting adults in private be no longer a criminal offence' (para. 62). Although the House of Lords debated homosexuality and prostitution—the two subjects dealt with by the Report—within three months of its appearance, there was no sign of active interest in the Commons and it became clear that the then Conservative Government had no desire to promote legislation along the recommended lines. Yet the Report had had a preponderantly sympathetic reception from the Press, Church spokesmen and professional organisations, and public opinion polls taken shortly after its appearance showed that some 40 per cent of the population accepted its findings while just over 50 per cent opposed them.

In the spring of 1958 there was a recurrence of old-style 'chain' prosecutions of consenting adult homosexuals at Assizes in various parts of the country. This directly precipitated the formation of the Homosexual Law Reform Society, which arose out of correspondence in various newspapers calling for active steps to promote the Wolfenden reforms. On 7 March 1958 the following letter appeared in *The Times*:

### HOMOSEXUAL ACTS

Sir,

We, the undersigned, would like to express our general agreement with the recommendation of the Wolfenden Report that homosexual acts committed in private between consenting adults should no longer be a criminal offence.

The present law is clearly no longer representative of either Christian or liberal opinion in this country, and now that there are widespread doubts about both its justice and its efficacy, we believe that its continued enforcement will do more harm than good to the health of the community as a whole.

The case for reform has already been accepted by most of the responsible newspapers and journals, by the two Archbishops, the Church Assembly, a Roman Catholic committee, a number of Non-Conformist spokesmen, and many other organs of public opinion.

In view of this, and of the conclusions which the Wolfenden Committee itself agreed upon after a prolonged study of the evidence, we should like to see the Government introduce legislation to give effect to the proposed reform at an early date; and are confident that if it does so it will deserve the widest support from humane men of all parties.

Yours, etc.,

N. G. ANNAN; ATTLEE; A. J. AYER; ISAIAH BERLIN; +LEONARD BIRMINGHAM; ROBERT BOOTHBY; C. M. BOWRA; C. D. BROAD; DAVID CECIL; L. JOHN COLLINS; ALEX COMFORT; A. E. DYSON; +ROBERT EXON; GEOFFREY FABER; JACQUETTA HAWKES; TREVOR HUDDLESTON CR; JULIAN HUXLEY; C. DAY LEWIS; W. R. NIBLETT; J. B. PRIESTLEY; RUSSELL; DONALD O. SOPER; STEPHEN SPENDER; MARY STOCKS; A. J. P. TAYLOR; E. M. W. TILLYARD; ALEC R. VIDLER; KENNETH WALKER; LESLIE D. WEATHERHEAD; C. V. WEDGWOOD; ANGUS WILSON; JOHN WISDOM; BARBARA WOOTTON.

Notwithstanding the distinction of the letter's signatories, the Government showed no inclination to take their advice. On 19 April *The Times* published a further letter supporting the Wolfenden recommendations, signed by fifteen eminent married women. Most of the signatories to these two letters, together with others who were now approached by A. E. Dyson (the university lecturer who was the moving spirit in forming the HLRS) became founder-members of the Society's 100-strong Honorary Committee—a very distinguished band which was somewhat sourly referred to by one of the London evening papers as 'the pick of the lilac establishment'. A smaller executive committee, with the late Kenneth Walker—a well-known surgeon and sexologist—as Chairman, began planning a political campaign. As Mr Walker has put it, 'We all agreed that the law as it stood was archaic, grossly unfair and ineffective. Some of us would have put the matter far more strongly than this' *(Sexual Behaviour, Creative and Destructive,* Kimber, 1966, p. 242).

During its early months the Society had no permanent office, and the bulk of its clerical work was done by voluntary helpers at the home of two of them. (As these two were, in fact, living together in a homosexual relationship, their action in letting the Society use their address was as brave as their work for it over a period of years was efficient and dedicated.) By the autumn, enough funds had been collected to enable a paid Secretary to be appointed and an office to be opened. The Revd A. Hallidie Smith became the Society's first Secretary at 32 Shaftesbury Avenue, W1, which remained its headquarters for the entire reform campaign.

This much success brought its own problems. Previously the Society's contact with supporters and other members of the public had been almost entirely through correspondence. Now, with an office to be telephoned and visited, the volume of work descending upon the Secretary rocketed—not least in the form of unscheduled callers with personal problems, many of them urgently requiring advice and practical help. This aspect of the work has always consumed a great deal (some would say too much) of the staff's time and energies. The Press, too, demanded information and articles. Various organisations and groups requested a speaker. Soon the office was overburdened (a state which remained chronic throughout my own tenure, despite a staff expansion which at its peak in 1965–67 totalled seven full-time paid employees), while the voluntary helpers' team was still coping with most of the routine enquiries. This not unnaturally led to criticisms of the office; internal dissensions were happily rare within the HLRS, but it has not always been plain sailing for the incumbent of the 'hot seat', whose critics usually have little conception of the pressures involved in running an intensely busy, precariously financed operation of this sort. (Money is a recurring headache for all voluntary organisations. My own view is that responsibility for raising it should be assumed by the governing body—if necessary through a separate fund-raising com-committee—and should not be imposed upon the chief executive, who has his hands more than full carrying out the day-to-day work of campaigning. At the height of the law reform activity in Parliament, I found myself having to spend almost half my time extracting funds from sympathisers to avoid the Society's imminent collapse at a time when it was in daily consultation with many members of both Houses of Parliament).

Readers of this essay will doubtless be familiar with the limitations placed by the Charities Acts upon political activities. This presents problems for campaigning organisations whose primary purpose is to ameliorate social problems and who seek changes in the law towards this end. As I have already mentioned, the HLRS found itself operating willy-nilly as a social casework agency from the time its office opened. In order to qualify for charitable grants and tax relief in connection with this side of its work, some executive committee members formed the Albany Trust, a registered charity whose objects are 'to promote psychological health in men by collecting data and conducting research; to publish the results thereof by writing, films, lectures and other media; to take suitable steps based thereon for the public benefit; to improve social and general conditions necessary for such healthy psychological development'. As time passed, the functions of the Albany Trust became more extensive than those of the HLRS and were by their nature more long-term, if not permanent. After the reform Bill became law, the HLRS was more or less dormant, but the Albany Trust saw new horizons of social work ahead. Yet the mistaken notion that the reform of 1967 had largely 'solved' the problems of homosexuals obscured this fact in many quarters which ought to have been better informed, with the result that the Trust is now burdened with a case-load of some. 3000 people a year which is still growing, while its income has declined.

This points to the need for continuous education of the public as to all aspects of the problem with which one is dealing. To oversimplify by crystallising upon a single issue, such as the passage of a Parliamentary Bill, is sometimes unavoidable but may in some ways be counter-productive.

The second phase of the Society's life stretched from the autumn of 1958 through to mid-1964. It might be labelled 'the long haul'. The Society's executive committee realised that there was little immediate hope of legislation. The Home Secretary Mr R. A. Butler (as he then was), had said in the first Commons 'Wolfenden' debate in November 1958 that time was needed to educate the public towards general acceptance of the Report's recommendations, and the Society regarded itself as the chief instrument of public education. At this stage it mostly kept away from Parliament and concentrated upon the Press and the public. The circulation of its pamphlet *Homosexuals and the Law* to all MPs before the 1958 debate, coinciding as it did with similar distributions (unknown to it) from other sources of Peter Wildeblood's book *Against the Law* and Eustace Chesser's *Live and Let Live,* had given rise to a Parliamentary outcry by opponents of reform that the House was being subjected to the rich attentions of 'a rich and powerful lobby of perverts' (who never existed: if they had, the Society's task might have been less hazardous. In fact, the mythical cohorts of wealthy 'queers' eagerly pouring money into the Society's coffers remained mythical). One result of this scare was that the MPs on the Society's executive—notably Mr Kenneth Robinson (later to be Minister of Health)—advised strongly against any further early direct approaches to the Commons, as the debate of November 1958 had made it quite apparent that early legislation could not be expected. As Kenneth Walker has written:

'It was clear . . . that a long and arduous fight lay ahead. To "educate" the public upon such an emotional topic as homosexuality to the extent that the Wolfenden proposals might become palatable to politicians who feared, apparently, a massive constituency backlash from those who were totally ignorant of the subject, was a formidable task for a small and slenderly financed voluntary organisation such as the HLRS. Nevertheless, we set out to obtain as much publicity as possible for the need to change this law, and The Revd Hallidie Smith . . . began addressing numerous meetings of constituency political parties, university societies and discussion groups ranging from Church organisations to humanists—an activity which its successors have continued at an increasing tempo. I believe that there have now been hundreds of such meetings addressed by representatives of the Society, and that at not one of them has a predominantly hostile audience been encountered. Indeed, motions in favour of homosexual law reform are repeatedly carried in university unions and debating societies up and down the country, and not a single one has been lost. So much for "public opinion" as we have encountered it face to face. In press correspondence, too, the letters published are predominantly in favour of reform. With one or two exceptions, opponents of the Wolfenden recommendations are remarkably inarticulate and unwilling to engage in public discussion of the matter.'
                                                                    (Op. cit. p. 244)

The next Parliamentary airing of the Wolfenden proposals was in June 1960, when Mr Kenneth Robinson took an early opportunity following the 1959 general election to move a Commons Motion calling on the Government 'to take an early action' on the Report's recommendations. Despite a number of strongly sympathetic speeches (mostly from the Labour side), the Home Secretary, Mr Butler, again made a temporising speech and the motion was defeated by 213 votes to 99. But even some of its opponents admitted in their speeches that reform must eventually come.

This debate was the first major occasion for the HLRS to practise the techniques of supporting a Parliamentary initiative; a 'trial run', as it were, for the main campaign of 1965–67. The Society's activities in this respect have been flatteringly described in some quarters as 'sophisticated'. I would prefer to characterise them as 'discreet'. What we did—then and later—never amounted to a mass lobbying operation of the blunderbuss variety which some organisations assume (wrongly, in my view) to be required: we had learned somewhat painfully from the 1958 debate that blanket circulations of all MPs are almost certainly a mistake. Consequently, we were largely guided in what we did by the advice and requests of our chief Parliamentary sponsors—at this stage Mr Robinson, later Lord Arran and Mr Leo Abse. We endeavoured to carry out, to the best of our ability, what they required of us. This involved the supplying of information which they needed and, when necessary, research into points of detail; there were also a good deal of routine clerical work in connection with the 'whipping' letters which they personally circulated to their voting supporters before each debate, the keeping of comprehensive lists of all MPs on record as having spoken or voted in favour or of against homosexual law reform, and so forth—but very rarely the making of direct approaches by the HLRS to Members of either House who were not already known to us. As a result, those who wished to help (and on some occasions even those who opposed the reform!) tended to come to the Society for information; so that by 1966 we probably had a much wider range of Parliamentary contacts than we would have acquired by 'badgering' unknown MPs out of the blue.

This combination of assiduous but quiet rallying of support within Parliament by the Bill's sponsors there, assisted by our office acting as 'general staff', proved singularly effective. I am sure that any attempt by the HLRS to operate independently of the Parliamentarians (a role which some pressure groups aspire to) would have been a mistake, both in principle and in practice. There were occasions during the Bill's passage when the Society could have wished that more attention had been paid to its viewpoint; but these were genuine differences of opinion about what was practicable rather than disagreements as to ends, and the degree of understanding and smooth co-operation between the Parliamentary and extra-Parliamentary wings of the reform movement remained generally close throughout.

The month before Mr Robinson's debate the Society had held its first (and largest ever) public meeting at the Caxton Hall (on 12 May, the second anniversary of the Society's foundation). Despite some difficulties—later to become tediously familiar—over advertising, enough posters and handbills were distributed before the event to produce an audience of well over 1000, and an overflow meeting had to be hastily arranged in one of the smaller halls in the building in addition to the main one. Speakers included the Bishop of Exeter, Mrs Anne Allen JP, the late Mr Kingsley Martin, Dr Neustatter and The Revd A. Hallidie Smith. The meeting was interesting in that it revealed a wide variety of attitudes about homosexuality and towards homosexuals, both among the speakers and members of the audience: yet all agreed that the legal reforms supported by the Society were necessary. The Bishop of Exeter's description of the then prevailing law as 'a monstrous injustice' summed up the feeling of the meeting, which with only three dissentients carried a resolution urging the Government to implement the Wolfenden findings 'without further delay'. Immediately after the meeting, a letter signed by the Chairman and Secretary was written to the Home Secretary, in which the result of the meeting and the predominantly favourable reception given to the Society's campaign throughout the country was recorded. Mr Butler replied before the June debate that he still considered legislation would be 'premature'. Despite the meeting's success, it received hardly any press publicity: the time had not yet come when homosexuality and homosexual law reform was regarded by the Press as a topic of general interest.

The next bout of reformist activity came somewhat later in the same Parliament, in March 1962, when Mr Leo Abse (Labour MP for Pontypool, and already well known for his interest in social causes) introduced a Sexual Offences Bill which deliberately omitted any reference to the controversial legislation of homosexual acts between consenting adults in private but sought to enact some of the subsidiary proposals of the Wolfenden Committee—to ensure that men complaining of homosexual blackmail should not themselves be prosecuted, that 'stale' charges relating to homosexual offences more than 12 months old should be prohibited, and that all cases against 'consenting adults in private' should be brought, if at all, by the Director of Public Prosecutions. This attempt to mollify the main current of opposition with legal compromise met with little favour; the Bill was 'talked out' by opponents who were as vehement against it as if it had embodied the main Wolfenden proposal. They wanted none of what one of them called 'Wolfenden watered down'. Another objected to these 'abominable' offences being muddled up with 'more respectable' sexual crimes in the Bill's title, and expressed the hope that neither that nor any future Parliament would go one inch along the path of legalising homosexuality, which he described as 'particularly repugnant to the vast majority of people in this country'.

Notwithstanding such extreme views, it became known in July 1964 that the Director of Public Prosecutions had 'requested'

Chief Constables to consult him before prosecuting men for homosexual acts committed in private with another consenting adult, and also in respect of offences more than 12 months old or revealed because of blackmail complaints. It was pointed out by the Attorney-General at the time, and also by Home Office spokesmen in subsequent Parliamentary debates, that this did not imply that any change in the law had taken place through administrative action, or that the law was never to be applied against consenting adults. Nevertheless, this directive (whose cause remains somewhat obscure) was the first sign of official concern at the operation of the existing law.

It had been preceded, in the spring of 1964, by another Parliamentary initiative—the last of that Parliament—from an unexpectedly right-wing quarter. Sir Thomas Moore, the High Tory MP for Ayr and 'father' of the House of Commons, was usually regarded as an extreme supporter of the death penalty and of corporal punishment. But he was a supporter of the Wolfenden proposals because, as he once told me, he had known some men of upright character whose lives had been made miserable because of this law. As a result of a summary of case histories circulated by the Society at the end of 1963, he asked the Home Secretary (Mr Brooke) when he proposed implementing the Wolfenden Report; and on receiving a negative reply, Sir Thomas tabled a Motion in April 1964 calling on the Government to legislate on the grounds that this 'would tend to prevent much danger of blackmail and many personal tragedies'. He requested the Society to ask those MPs who had supported Kenneth Robinson in 1960 to sign his Motion, but only about two dozen did so: several of them considered that it was too near the end of Parliament's life for such a gesture to be fruitful; others may have been unwilling to march under Sir Thomas's banner. He himself was disappointed at the paucity of support, and privately expressed the view that with a general election in the offing, those with marginal seats were unwilling to sign anything which might have been used against them in the forthcoming campaign. As he was retiring from Parliament, he had no need to worry. Nevertheless, his initiative may have played some part in bringing about the Director of Public Prosecutions' subsequent directive; in any event, Sir Thomas Moore (who died recently) deserves an honourable mention in the annals of homosexual law reform.

The opponents of reform remained in a majority (though a much smaller one) in the Parliament of 1964–66. Mr Abse's 'half-way'

Bill had convincingly demonstrated that opposition to even minor alterations to the law would be just as strenuous as to a 'whole-hog' measure, and the Society accordingly decided that it would endeavour to obtain a sponsor for a full Wolfenden reform as soon as possible after the general election of October 1964. This brought Labour into power, but with such a tiny majority that a further general election within a few months seemed inevitable, and the MPs on the HLRS executive were dubious as to the usefulness of a full-scale Parliamentary Effort before this took place. However, the Earl of Arran got in touch with the Society soon after the new Parliament met and said he intended to take an early opportunity of raising the question of the Wolfenden reforms in the House of Lords. Lord Arran had never been (and never became) a member of either the Honorary Committee or the HLRS executive, and acted quite independently and on his own initiative, taking full and final responsibility for all the decisions which he had to make, although he consulted closely with us throughout the campaign which now commenced. There is no doubt that the main Parliamentary credit for achieving homosexual law reform is his; for while the Bill would not have got through the Commons without Leo Abse's skillful tactical generalship, it was Lord Arran's dogged perseverance and sensitivity to the mood of the Upper House in 1965 and 1966 which paved the way to ultimate success in 1967.

This was not Lord Arran's first sortie into the field of homosexual law reform; before the general election he had written to the then Prime Minister (Sir Alec Douglas-Home) urging the case for implementation of the Wolfenden proposals by the Conservative Party in the interests of compassion and personal freedom, but he had received a discouraging reply: this was not a nettle which Conservatives cared to grasp. However, with a new Government in office and an influx of younger, more radically minded MPs, Lord Arran felt that an initiative in the Lords would be worthwhile. He was right. On 12 May 1965 his Motion 'drawing attention' to the Wolfenden Committee's report on homosexuality (which the Peers had not debated since 1958) was supported by a distinguished array of speakers including the two Archbishops; sixteen Peers spoke in favour of reform whilst only three opposed it. The Labour Government's spokesman maintained neutrality, as his Conservative predecessors had done—but this time a positive neutrality rather than a negative one, with clear hints that if the House took a favourable decision in favour of reform the Government would not seek to frustrate its wish. The form of the motion precluded a vote, but two weeks later a simple one-clause Bill tabled by Lord Arran, providing that homosexual behaviour between consenting adults in private should not be a criminal offence, was given a Second Reading by 94 votes to 49. This symbolic victory of almost two to one signalled a breakthrough, and was a personal triumph for Lord Arran. With drafting help from the Government, he steered a full Bill embodying the substance of all the Wolfenden Committee's recommendations through its detailed Committee and Report stages to receive its Third Reading in October 1965 by 116 votes to 46.

Inevitably, there were some minor setbacks. The Bill's opponents tabled a series of 'wrecking' amendments, and succeeded in carrying one of these—a much narrower definition of 'in private' than that envisaged by the Wolfenden Committee—into the Bill. (The Committee had contemplated that whether a homosexual act was 'in private' or not should be decided by the courts, *pari passu* with their decisions in heterosexual cases of behaviour alleged to be offensive to public decency; the Act as finally passed provides that a homosexual act is regarded as not 'in private'—and therefore remains unlawful—'when more than two persons take part or are present', thereby substituting a quite different concept.) On a number of other points, the Government's draft clauses differed from what the Society would have liked. But Lord Arran was not willing to jeopardise the continuation of Government assistance in the provision of technical advice and Parliamentary time, so that the Society asked other supporters of the Bill to table amendments embodying its views. These—notably one on conspiracy, ably moved by Lady Wootton on two occasions—covered some important legal points and produced interesting discussions, but were generally not successful because of Home Office opposition. This resistance was usually in fact to the substance of the amendments, but most of the objections were ostensibly directed to what was said to be their 'defective drafting': so in the result the Government got its way in a somewhat backhanded manner (especially as it was officially 'neutral' towards the Bill). Lord Arran, as he was fully entitled to do, preferred their views on most of these points to those of the Society, but it was unfortunate that he somewhat too readily assumed a lack of technical competence on our part in drafting clauses which in fact embodied principles which the Government were unwilling to accept—though they were frequently in closer accord with the recommendations of the Wolfenden Committee than the final terms of the Bill. It was also disappointing and somewhat frustrating to the Society that at no time were they invited by either Lord Arran or Mr Abse to a drafting conference with the Parliamentary draftsman who assisted in drawing up the Bill. Perhaps as a consequence of this omission, it is noteworthy that all the points at which the 1967 Sexual Offences Act departs from the letter of the Wolfenden recommendations are in a more restrictive direction than that envisaged by the Committee.

These, however, are comparatively trivial discomfitures when set against the great achievement of passing the Bill; and I only mention them at all in order to demonstrate that 'pressure groups'—even well-organised ones—are by no means omnipotent in relation to the Parliamentary sponsors of legislation in which they have an interest. Even the friendliest and best-disposed of sponsors rightly tend to emphasise that the final decisions as to Parliamentary tactics and terms must be their prerogative. Politics is 'the art of the possible' although there is room for legitimate differences of opinion as to what is in fact possible in any given situation. Where such differences occur, those within Parliament, and not those outside it, must inevitably have the last word.

In contrast to the Peers, the Commons remained reluctant to accept reform. In May 1965, two days after the Second Reading of Lord Arran's Bill, MPs refused Mr Abse leave to bring in a similar Bill under the Ten-Minute Rule by 178 votes to 159—a significantly different hostile majority (19 votes) to the 114 of 1960. Public opinion was also swinging in the right direction. National Opinion and Gallup Polls published in the autumn showed that over 60 per cent of the respondents now agreed that homosexual behaviour between consenting adults in private should no longer be a criminal offence. This change in the balance of opinion since 1959 followed an intensive phase of Press publicity and public speaking, in most of which the HLRS was directly involved. Since the spring of 1964, Press requests for information and articles had multiplied, and numerous speaking engagements were undertaken. The Press 'breakthrough' came, in my estimation, when within a few weeks of each other three of the most prominent women journalists in the country approached the Society saying that they wished to write about homosexuality as they felt it was time that the veil of genteel ignorance was ripped from their female readers' eyes. They did so, frankly and sympathetically; and this successful invasion of mums' and girlfriends' magazines started a process of more forthright dealing with sexual topics in their columns which has continued ever since. In the public speaking field, a great many university debates occurred on the Wolfenden proposals during 1964, 1965 and 1966, in most of which HLRS spokesmen participated and in none of which were the reformers defeated. Usually they won by overwhelming majorities. (Their opponents were, indeed, hard put to it to find coherent arguments for retaining the *status quo.* Sometimes they themselves could not be found, and at least one debate took place in which the leading 'opponent' was in fact a supporter of reform who stood in at the last moment for a bashful 'anti' M.P.)

Lord Arran's Bill had only passed through the Upper House when the session ended, and it was therefore necessary for it to pass again through all its stages in both Houses in order to become law (there being a convention that all legislation dies if it is still 'in the pipeline' at the end of the annual Parliamentary session). Immediately the new Parliamentary year started in November, therefore, Lord Arran reintroduced his Bill in the Lords. In the Commons there was also a new and more hopeful start: Mr Humphry Berkeley, the Conservative MP for Lancaster, drew second place in the annual ballot for Private Members' Bills and announced his intention of introducing a Commons Bill similar to Lord Arran's. He did so in close consultation with the HLRS, and after a five-hour debate his Bill succeeded in obtaining its Second Reading by 164 votes to 107 on 11 February 1966, after a speech from the Labour Home Secretary, Mr Roy Jenkins, expressing his forthright support for the measure (in marked contrast to his predecessors' hesitant stance). Unfortunately, after this promising start, national politics supervened and Parliament was dissolved in March 1966 so that the Sexual Offences Bills in both Houses automatically lapsed.

When the new Parliament, which had a substantial Labour majority, met, Lord Arran once again introduced his Bill in the Lords. It was given its Second Reading on 26 April by 70 votes to 29, its Third Reading on 16 June by 83 votes to 39 and passed by 78 votes to 60. Leo Abse now brought his (identical) Bill into the Commons under the Ten-Minute Rule procedure: it was approved by 244 votes to 100, the size of the reformist vote reflecting the more liberal views of the new intake of younger Labour and Conservative members. (About 60 Conservatives consistently voted for the Bill and ensured its majority throughout its passage.) This victory, and the moral support of the Lords' votes, enabled Mr Abse to secure enough Government time to permit the Bill to pass through all its remaining stages in the Commons. The Second Reading debate took place on 19 December, technically without a division, although a vote on a procedural Motion to enable the debate to continue after 10 p.m. obtained the support of 194 members against 84. Mr Abse's next success was in persuading the Government business managers to appoint a separate Standing Committee for the Bill so that it would not be held up in the queue of Private Members' Bills already waiting to be examined by the Standing Committee assigned to deal with them, and which was currently wrestling with the lengthy intricacies of the Abortion Bill. Mr Abse's Bill passed through its Committee stage at a single sitting on 19 April 1967—a remarkable feat in striking contrast with the marathon Committee stage wrangles which had held up the Abortion Bill for three months and were threatening to jeopardise its passage into law. In order to avoid a repetition of this state of affairs, Mr Abse's supporters deliberately avoided a lengthy discussion of amendments; while the opponents were nearly all absent from the Committee's first and only sitting. Nevertheless, some important amendments were made to the Bill in Committee, and a number of controversial points were aired—several of them by supporters of the Bill at the HLRS's behest, notably that of the age of consent: 21, many of us felt, was too high to be realistic and the penalties laid down by the Bill for committing homosexual acts below that age were too severe. Such a law, said the Hon Nicholas Ridley (Conservative, Cirencester and Tewkesbury), would make no sense at all in the minds of the young men of generations to come who would grow up being expected to observe it, and it would be a disaster to make a mistake over this. Mr Abse, however, stood firm for 21 and another influential member of the Commons who supported a lower age (Mr G. R. Strauss, Labour, Vauxhall) urged his colleagues to suppress their doubts and worries about some of the Bill's details at this stage of its precarious life so as to ensure its passage onto the Statute Book.

One major new clause—inserted with Mr Abse's agreement to mollify the only organised lobby of opponents which had manifested itself during the most recent series of House of Lords debates—exempted the Merchant Navy from the provisions of the Bill. Representatives of the National Maritime Board and of the National Union of Seamen had had discussions with Mr Abse and their spokesmen had objected to his Bill on Second Reading on the grounds that it failed to provide a similar degree of 'protection' for merchant seamen to that given to members of the armed services (whose complete exemption from the benefits conferred upon civilians by the Bill ran counter to the recommendations of the Wolfenden Committee but had been accepted by Mr Abse to meet the belated wishes of the Service Ministries, who had abandoned their earlier position of neutrality and moved to a more restrictive attitude). Somewhat to the surprise of the Bill's opponents, Mr Abse had, between Second Reading and Committee stage, acquiesced to the insertion of a new clause—now Section 2 of the Act—whose effect was to provide that a homosexual act between two consenting adults in private remained an offence if committed on a United Kingdom merchant ship between a crew member of that ship and another crew member of the same or of any other United Kingdom merchant ship. That fact that such acts, if done on board a ship by a member of its crew with a passenger or a foreign merchant seaman, are apparently not illegal under the terms of the clause, seems to have escaped its supporters! (Although Mr Ben Whitaker (Labour, Hampstead), who favoured the Bill as a whole, pointed out the illogicality of the new clause and said it would bring the whole of English law into ridicule.) The HLRS remained a passive and somewhat bemused spectator of this seafaring skirmish, which was conducted virtually singlehanded by Mr Abse; it was a highly successful tactical foray on his part, which successfully drew the sting of opposition to the Bill at its Committee stage.

The opposition, however, rallied for the Report stage and kept up a determined fillibuster throughout the extra Friday allotted by the Government. Strong pressure brought upon the Leader of the House by the Bill's friends (strengthened by the Home Secretary's sympathetic attitude towards it) enabled the debate to be resumed after 10 p.m. on Monday, 3 July, and after an all-night sitting it was given a Third Reading by 99 votes to 14. In all, there had been thirteen divisions during the Report stage, and on four occasions Mr Abse's supporters successfully voted the closure, which necessitated the presence of at least 100 of them; the opponents never exceeded 40. Mr Abse's Bill was then sent to the Lords, who gave it a Second Reading by 111 votes to 48 and formally passed it through its remaining stages to receive the Royal Assent on 27 July 1967. As a chronicler of this and other social reforms of the 1966–70 Parliament has written: 'To secure the enactment of a major Bill is a great political achievement for a back-bencher'.* The Sexual Offences Act of 1967 was the joint achievement of Lord Arran and Mr Leo Abse, both of whom combined persistence with Parliamentary skill to a marked degree.

How satisfactory was the campaign from the HLRS's point of view ? Personally, I have always regarded the legislative process as a fundamental part of public education, and there is no doubt that the series of Parliamentary debates between 1965 and 1967 helped considerably to educate the public mind about the existence and nature of homosexuality, although a high degree of ignorance still remained after the law was changed. As Professor Richards has pointed out, 'a feature of the Parliamentary debates on this subject is that the fundamental moral issue was consistently avoided'. Practically without exception, supporters of the reform conceded that homosexual acts were intrinsically undesirable, and some maintained that they were unnatural. Is this really true ? A frank debate was not forthcoming because (to quote Professor Richards again) 'clearly it was not in the interest of the reformers to raise contentious issues of this sort. Their task was to arouse Christian compassion, not Christian controversy. Their tactic was to keep public and Parliamentary debate as rational and moderate as possible because of the danger that an upsurge of emotion and prejudice would ruin their chance of success.'

As a consequence of this continuing unwillingness of politicians to face up to the needs, in the first instance for any action at all, and subsequently for a really frank and searching debate, the discussions which did take place in Parliament between 1965 and 1967 contained elements of unreality and to that extent were in fact irrational. How far could the course of these debates have been influenced by more effective (or different) tactics on the part of the HLRS ? I do not believe very much. The Society's chief contribution had been made before the debates of 1965 began, in creating the climate of opinion in which they could be held at all. It is perhaps in the nature of pressure groups that this should be so. Once an issue comes before Parliament, its Parliamentary sponsors take charge—and they are unlikely to pay undue attention to outside influences (even friendly ones) unless they are

* Professor Peter G. Richards: *Parliament and Conscience* (Allen and Unwin, 1970).

unusually modest or timid souls, in which case they would be unlikely to be piloting a Bill through Parliament. Indeed, there is a discernible tendency on the part of most MPs and Peers to discount organised opinion from any quarter, just because it *is* organised. Perhaps this betrays a subconscious resentment on their part of the nowadays all but universal Party Whip.

What, then, were the salient features of the homosexual law reform campaign, seen from the Homosexual Law Reform Society's standpoint? First and foremost, I would say that the more intensive a pressure group is, the more it experiences a sensation of pressures being focused upon itself—from friends as well as from opponents.In the early days, the pressures derived from being virtually the sole channel of reforming activity, from 1958 until 1964, and the brunt of opinion-forming (in accordance with Mr Butler's behest) was compounded by the intensive pressures imposed by a growing number of individuals direly in need of help: a facet of the work which was maintained and indeed grew throughout the busiest period of Parliamentary work. The phase of active reform brought new insights, some new frustrations, but also an elevating sense of achievement which sustained all concerned. The frustrations derived from the realisation that the Society's efforts were undeniably essential, but nevertheless not central enough in the minds of the Bill's Parliamentary champions to mould either the tactics of debate or the detailed shape of the resulting legislation as much as we might have wished. (But their hands, too, were tied by the need to ensure that Government 'neutrality' was benevolent as regards the provision of debating time and drafting assistance.)

The resulting blurring of certain issues led (as Professor Richards has pointed out) to a less satisfactory reform than might otherwise have been achieved—notably in its civil liberties aspects, where the desirable and equitable objective of equality before the law for homosexuals and heterosexuals was negated in several additional respects beyond those conceded by the Wolfenden Committee. One particular unfortunate failure was the lack of Government response to Lady Wootton's amendments (twice tabled at the HLRS's request) seeking to ensure that conspiracy charges should not be brought against people committing, seeking to commit, or facilitating, homosexual acts legalised by the Act. The forseeable outcome of this has been the 'conspiracy to corrupt public morals' charges recently brought (successfully) against the publishers of *International Times* and (unsuccessfully) against those of *OZ*. In this and other respects (notably with regard to the age of consent; the heavy penalties still incurred by some homosexual behaviour between consenting parties if one of them is under 21; the complete exclusion of Scotland, Northern Ireland and serving members of the Armed Forces from the benefits of the reform; and the restrictive definition of 'in private') the 1967 Sexual Offences Act stands itself in need of amendment.

But I should like, in conclusion, to make it plain that in saying this I am expressing a personal opinion rather than a collective HLRS one (because the Society's successor, the Sexual Law Reform Society, is still making a detailed study of further changes in the law which it may wish to propose); and that I in no way wish to derogate from the signal achievement of Lord Arran and Mr Abse. Theirs was the brunt and theirs the victory. We at the Society helped as we could—and in the event, I hope, not too clumsily. Whether or not the Act which our combined efforts obtained is destined to be an enduring solution, it was at least the first and essential step along the road towards a greater degree of justice and humanity in our sexual laws and *mores*.

# SHELTER
## BRIAN FROST and IAN HENDERSON

The irruption of 'Shelter', the national campaign for the homeless, on the scene in November, 1966, coinciding as it did with the showing of Jeremy Sandford's film *Cathy Come Home* about homelessness seen through the eyes of one family, caused immediate response from the British public. But the interest which this pressure group—and movement: for it was both—caused can be understood only if its roots are carefully traced over the whole of the 1960s.

For some years before 1966 there had been growing Christian concern about homelessness, seemingly on the increase, linked with the exposure of conditions in places like Newington Lodge by people like Audrey Harvey in her book on homelessness (Penguin, 1962).

In March 1961 the Bishops of Southwark and London led a procession from Southwark Cathedral to St Paul's Cathedral to draw attention to the problem. The Revd Bruce Kenrick (who had previously been involved in East Harlem) was spurred on by the bad housing conditions in Notting Hill to found the Notting Hill Housing Trust. Attention had already been focused on this area by the Profumo scandal in the latter days of the Macmillan administration; for Rachman, one of the property speculators involved in the scandal, had been in the habit of buying up old property and letting it at exorbitant rents, with concomitant over-population. At the same time as this activity was being generated from both underground and establishment pressures, there appeared a number of voluntary movements concerned with housing, linked in the National Federation of Housing Societies.

The downfall of Rachman gave the language a new word—'Rachmanism'—symbolising bad housing, overcrowding and exploitation of tenants by landlords. No one, however, quite saw how to handle the situation. There was much groping round for a solution, for something to focus the growing concern over housing from a number of quarters. 1963 saw the creation of the Christian Action 'Homeless in Britain' fund; plans were at the same time being generated in the Social Responsibility Department of the British Council of Churches for the creation of what came to be called The British Churches' Housing Trust, involving the Roman Catholic Church and the Jewish Community as well as the member churches of the Council. The 'Housing the Homeless Central Fund', another body in this field, also had strong Roman Catholic connections.

Yet another thread was the Catholic Housing Aid Society in which Maisie Ward, joint founder of the publishers Sheed and Ward, was involved. They recruited an Irishman who was chaplain to Irish immigrants in Slough, a dynamic man called Father Eamon Casey. He soon introduced into the housing question pastoral counselling—homeless families, he averred, needed advice; couples buying houses needed help in foreseeing the snags and difficulties which might occur.

It would be a mistake, however, to assume that these various groups had the same objectives. Some contained units of political agitation; others saw it as their task to provide alternative accommodation to 'Part 3' accommodation; still others to build up local housing associations. Some tried to buy up a substantial number of houses and redo them and let them to people in need.

There was, however, in these different groups—The Notting Hill Housing Trust, The Christian Action Housing in Britain Fund, The British Churches' Housing Trust and the Catholic agencies—one seed which was destined to be the most helpful. Contained in Christian Action's approach, it was never developed by them on a large scale; it was simply not to start more and more housing associations, but to look round for viable, exciting projects and put money into them, because such pump-priming money enabled them to get statutory grants.

At the beginning of 1966 the public of Britain was already beginning to respond to housing problems, partly as a result of the Notting Hill Housing Trust's large-scale, horrific advertising in the national papers. Housing concerns were learning to cut new ground. The same year the National Federation of Housing Associations called a meeting of people in the housing field, at which the Notting Hill Trust was prominent, with the suggestion that a national charity be established. This suggestion was put before a representative group of people made up of promotional experts and the housing societies. At the meeting a report on Britain's housing, broken down ward by ward over the biggest cities, was considered. Its author was an unknown man from New Zealand, a journalist called Des Wilson.

The suggestion was taken up and Shelter, the national campaign for the homeless, was created by five other groups—The British Churches' Housing Trust, The Notting Hill

Housing Trust, The Catholic Housing Aid Society. The National Federation of Housing Societies, The Christian Action 'Homeless in Britain' Fund—which agreed to let Shelter do their advertising and money-raising for them, Shelter then giving them grants to continue their work.

It decided to concentrate on four areas of major urban blight in housing: London, especially Notting Hill; Glasgow; Birmingham; and Liverpool. A short list of housing associations in these areas was drawn up. By now there was ample evidence from the Milner-Holland Report, published earlier; the Grieve Report on London's homeless; the academic papers of John Westergaard, from the London School of Economics; the Christian Action report on Glasgow; and the embryo Shelter housing reports, ward by ward, focusing especially on the appropriateness of or the misuse of the words' homelessness' and 'the homeless'. There were few people actually 'homeless' compared with the vast number of people living in ghastly conditions and with bad housing as a daily nagging nightmare. Some slum dwellers moved from place to place each six months. The Ministry of Housing, as it then was, estimated that three million people were living in houses condemned as unfit for human habitation. The early Shelter was not in fact concerned with homelessness. It was concerned about slum property. It spoke up for people its newly-appointed Director called 'the hidden homeless.'

It's Director was a man who had been conversant for a number of years with the world of public relations. Indeed the early days of Shelter, financed from a grant from The Notting Hill Housing Trust, relied on his flair and, originally, the advertising copy of one firm, Dunkeley and Freedlander. Coinciding as it did with *Cathy Come Home,* it could hardly have had a better start. But before that, for over three months, Wilson and his colleagues had been visiting and speaking to the journalists on all the national papers who they thought should be the people to write up their story. They treated the opening campaign to launch Shelter as a military operation, and impressed themselves on Fleet Street in a way that perhaps no other pressure group before or since had done in its early stages.

'This is a national emergency and in an emergency we all unite', its literature urged. For the duration of the launching of Shelter they used the word 'Christmas' wherever possible—'three million families in Britain will spend Christmas in slums', said their poster. The advertising agency also recommended shock tactics.

Even the full page advertisements in *The Times* were dominated by an enormous photograph, taking up at least two-thirds of the page, with the headline 'Home Sweet Hell'.

Des Wilson, who has written about the opening campaign of Shelter for an advertising magazine, wrote of his campaign: 'When we launched Shelter on December 1st it caught on immediately. Months of pressure and persuasion had worked. The Press, radio and TV coverage was greater than we could possibly have hoped for, despite such disappointments as losing "This Week" half an hour before they were due to start filming for the Thursday night. Nor did the Prime Minister's decision to meet Ian Smith on the "Tiger" do us any good. But many of the features were already in type.'

He considers the reasons for success in the early stages to be the timing—they started in June for a December launch; the choice of a few sharp catch phrases—'hidden homeless', 'rescue operations'; and a few basic facts—three million homeless. They planned and planned. They pursued a relentless person-to-person contact with journalists. They communicated their pace and sense of urgency to Fleet Street. Even though their direct-mail test was a failure they did not need to worry.

The story speaks for itself. Shelter, the National Campaign for the Homeless, was launched on 1 December 1966. In the first six weeks it brought in more than £70,000, was mentioned in the Press more than 150 times and on 25 different radio and television programmes. In a leader on 12 January 1967 the *Evening News* described the campaign as 'a triumph', The *Guardian* devoted two leaders to urging support for Shelter and even *The Times* devoted a leader to the campaign. Founder and Chairman to the Campaign was The Revd Bruce Kenrick, who master-minded the Notting Hill Housing Trust fund-raising campaign. His campaign director, Des Wilson, described the launch and explained the thinking behind the campaign in his article in the *Advertising Weekly,* 17 March 1967.

Which other pressure group or campaign had within such a short time so established itself as to warrant an article on its life and approach in a magazine such as the *Advertising Weekly*? Shelter had arrived with a bang, and with a brilliant director of personality and drive from an entirely different world from the usual recruitment areas of pressure groups and charities.

Shelter had been cultivating the Minister of Housing, Mr Greenwood. They were shortly to register another success. The housing subsidy was announced in the House of Commons on 9 November 1967. On that day the *Evening News* wrote: 'Shelter, whose campaign for Britain's homeless has reached £100,000 in 3 months, scored another success today. Their pressure forced a significant change in the Housing Subsidy Bill—enabling housing associations to acquire funds for buying old property. Originally, the Government's Bill was aimed at new homes and the improvement only of old properties. But during the committee stage, data and pressure from Shelter brought new thinking—plus written acknowledgement for their help from Housing Minister Mr Greenwood and Tory Opposition spokesmen. The present ceiling of local authority loans and grants is also raised from £800 to £2000.'

Shelter has also been an influence in all the political parties and has been supported by people of all parties. Indeed, it has gone out of its way to hold public meetings at the times of party conferences and to seek support from many MPs. Having done well with its political contacts, it also did well in approaching other specific groups: teachers, for evidence that children from bad homes found difficulty at school; the housing exhibition at Olympia and the women's magazines reporting on new homes, for information about attitude to their housing. It was Britain's newest and most famous pressure group, with a title which hardly bore relation to what it was doing—for the problems of vagrancy and actual homelessness were passing it by, with the pressures of bad housing, slums and degradation which its research was continuously uncovering, and with which it proceeded to castigate local authorities and regale the Press at the appropriate level of interest—story line, or facts. Its pressure group edge had built up well.

But all did not always go well. By 1967 Father Casey was Chairman and Des Wilson Director. The Director was given the right to be national spokesman to the Press and television. Within broad limits of policy this was a wise decision, because it meant that there could be no comment, when needed, on an issue which might at any time blow up. But what was Father Casey to do, for example, when the Director criticised Douglas Houghton, one of the most respected elder statesmen of the Labour Party, for a speech about family limitation? Father Casey was a Catholic priest and Houghton's views were opposed to the policy of his Church.

Sometimes Shelter's comment went off beam, but it did establish itself in the public mind as a pressure group for more resolute government in housing. It was a kind of watchdog. If evidence of this was needed, one had only to point to the success it met in recruiting young people to its ranks, especially from the cadres of Young Liberals, at that time immensely active. It was articulating a genuine collective political anger. Since the demise of the Campaign for Nuclear Disarmament there had been few groups which had so galvanised people, and Shelter filled this gap admirably. Its pragmatic style suited the time. But it was beginning to gain a number of enemies: both Tories and left-wing socialists were critical. However, the debate it stirred up—there was an Oxford Union debate with Des Wilson and Richard Crossman as two of the speakers—could only be healthy. Undoubtedly, there was an alignment with the poverty lobby. The Director was a member of the Child Poverty Action Group set up with specific and concrete political objectives, and numbering among its supporters some of the most eminent and experienced men in academic and research projects in Britain.

Despite criticisms from people like Evelyn King, Shelter went from strength to strength. One of its rallies in Trafalgar Square included statements about issues other than slums. It commented on other aspects of social poverty. It produced reports which sold well, but they were popular and lacked academic content.

And this raises the key question about Shelter: movement or pressure group? Effective, or riding the crest of the wave? Really influential, or only peripheral? Since the departure of Des Wilson from the Directorship, for example, it has seemed less forceful, though continuing to raise a lot of money. It has ceased to get its phenomenal Press coverage; ceased to be as contentious, although it had linked up in some measure with the Sqatters movement and intervened in some housing squabbles, such as a notorious one in the London Borough of Brent where the Council was acting in an arbitrary manner.

There is some truth in the assertion that Shelter is an ineffective establishment noise. It claims to have done this and that, but has it made more than a marginal improvement to the situation? Shelter would like to say that it has succeeded in making governments aware of the housing needs of people and, on occasion, in prodding bureaucracy,

By the start of the 1970s the radical movement had moved on and the housing issues were in the hands of the squatters. Shelter had cornered a share of the 'charity market'; like other charities it kept a wary eye on the charity commissioners, as doubtless the commissioners did on Shelter; but its first, fine, careless rapture had been dissipated. The honeymoon period was over. Moreover, what was its social philosophy ? The PR men had come and gone, it had launched a movement and opened people's eyes, but where was the focus to be ? Was it to be in seeing bad housing as part of the total problem of an environment, the community development point; was it to be patch-work, the helping of housing associations to buy this or that house; or what ? It was significant that when the Trustees met to consider taking a pioneer project for vagrants under its wings, it was felt that Shelter couldn't take on any more. It had to re-trench; it had to establish clear boundaries. Yet if ever there was an organisation which could have pioneered work in this direction, it was Shelter.

Shelter illustrates powerfully the problem that has faced a number of groups in Britain which have used pressure really effectively, yet have also been large and well-known charities. How can the two be combined ? In the end, does one become part of the scene, accepted and lacking bite and drive ? The powers at work in society tame the dog, domesticate him and learn to live with his style.

In a way, this is what has happened. The seeds of Shelter's success were sown in the late 1950s and early 1960s; its creation marked a high-water peak in Harold Wilson's Britain and provided an outlet for many who were politically frustrated with the greyness of the Wilson era. But where have they got in hard thinking and working out new housing policies ? To what extent have they really influenced the civil service mandarins and government officials in both major parties ?

It is hard to tell. It is significant, however, that Jeremy Sandford's attempt to do for the vagrant what he did for Cathy has not hit the headlines. For *Edna The Inebriate Woman*, his recently televised play, has had hardly any effect, other than a comparison with his other play. Perhaps Shelter missed the way when it turned down a special project on vagrancy; maybe its future lies in demonstration pilot housing projects in different parts of the country like the one it started in Liverpool, rather than in focusing on the limitless needs of the various housing associations up and down the country.

And that is a policy decision requiring a certain definite sharpness and edge, going beyond public relations and immediate responses to human need to social critique and long-term strategic and preventive aims. It is a tall order. Maybe Shelter's policy document 'Policy for the Homeless' will lead them in the right direction, and their new team can open up new areas to be explored.

# THE BIAFRA LOBBY

## BARBARA McCALLUM

In 1967 a civil war started in Nigeria which lasted for three years. During the war many countries became involved in sending or selling arms or food supplies and in diplomatic efforts to try to end it. Because of the long period of British involvement and the large amount of British business investment in Nigeria, Britain was in a very influential position, though other countries like America, France, Portugal and the Ivory Coast were also prominent in their support for one or other of the sides.

Throughout the war Britain favoured the Federal Government rather than the Government of the Republic of Biafra (the name used during the war years for that part of the people of Nigeria which broke away from the rest of the Federation). British policy was centred mainly on continuing to allow the sale of arms to Nigeria, which had traditionally relied on Britain for them.

During the previous two years there had been two military coups when the Ibos from the East were seen to be predominant, and a third when the mainly Northern and Western Nigerians were alternatively paramount in both power and influence. The massacres of Ibos living in the North a year before the war started led to many families in the East losing a relative, or receiving back to their already overcrowded area wounded relatives of those who were fit and ready to work, but for whom no work was available. This fact of the failure of the Federal Government to acknowledge the situation, together with the festering resentment in the East and the fact that ratification of the agreement made by the military leaders at Aburi in Ghana was not carried out, were major contributions to the start of the civil war. The division of the Federation of Nigeria into twelve states also disturbed many in the East.

The situation was complicated, as in most civil wars, by other factors. There had been long-standing jealousy and resentment of the Ibos, who were found all over the country and were noted for their aggressive business ability. To many they had appeared responsible for the first of the military coups. Some of the non-Ibo people living in the East were not really in favour of secession, but would have found it difficult to protest. The East was the main area, though not the only one, for oil interests, centred on the town of Port Harcourt where there was also a fairly recently built refinery. As mineral rights were the property of the Federal

Government, the Nigerians were obviously afraid of losing this income.

Unlike the situation in East Pakistan, the atrocities in the North of Nigeria received very little attention outside Nigeria; and so when the Easterns eventually seceded, the background was little understood, and the people who began to form a lobby to get the Government to change its policy found that very little was known. In contrast, the Bangla Desh supporters in 1971 may have found that the people in Britain understood something of the predicament of East Pakistan, although they may have been very ill-informed about the geographical facts and ethnic origin of the people in Bangla Desh and West Pakistan.

By the time something of the predicament of the Biafrans had been given publicity the main concern was the starvation of the people, especially the children. The leader of the Biafrans, General Ojukwu, was seen by many more as an obstacle to feeding the children than a leader with a cause, because he did not want food flown in by daylight; he knew that if relief flights at night stopped he could not be sure of getting a supply of arms through under cover of these flights.

The Biafra lobby—which was formed in 1967 and lasted till 1970—was unusually informed, and points to the fact that even an informed working group is no prerequisite for success. Members had either worked in Nigeria and knew the people, the terrain and facts and figures about the situation, or else made it their business to find out. They would not necessarily have wanted the East to leave the Federation, or have even been convinced that Biafra could win, but supported the lobby because of strong convictions that justice had not been done. In addition, there were a large number of sympathisers who were concerned about the question of starvation; who raised money for food but were not concerned about the political aspect of the war. The former group was concerned about the historical situation and the identity and future of the people as a whole. They were particularly critical of the role played by the British Government.

The Biafra group in Britain was disunited throughout, which lessened its chances of success; and the likelihood of changing the British Government's policy was small, as both the Opposition and the Government held the same view. There has only been one time in recent decades when the Government changed its attitude in a matter of foreign policy in the way the lobby hoped, and that was in the autumn of 1935 when Italy was invading Abyssinia and Sir Samuel Hoare was Foreign Secretary. Great Britain appealed to the League of Nations and certain sanctions were imposed. Early in 1936 Hoare visited Paris and made an agreement with Lavelle, and a peace proposal was put forward and made public that Italy should have a partial conquest. There was a great public outcry, the Liberal and Labour parties opposed Hoare and eventually Baldwin accepted Hoare's resignation.

There were many complications leading to the Government's support for Nigeria. One was the oil question: the supply of oil was already threatened in the Middle East with a potential Arab Israeli war. Analogies by some to the situation in Katanga and the American Civil War caused the Government too to back the Federal Nigerian side. Both sides of the House of Commons had an understandable fear of secession, as it was thought that if Biafra seceded, then groups in other countries (particularly in Africa) might do the same. The general Tory view was that General Ojukwu, the Biafran leader, was the root cause of the trouble. This, and lack of contact between reasonable Biafrans likely to be accepted by the British Establishment and Her Majesty's Government, was one of the major difficulties the pressure group faced in trying to get more dialogue going on in London about the civil war. There were fears, too, that Russia would greatly extend her influence in Nigeria and West Africa. If Russia had supported Biafra the situation might have been different, as Great Britain might not have wanted to oppose Russia openly to any great extent.

There were, however, MPs on both sides of the House of Commons who were particularly concerned with the Biafran cause, though they were back-bench members. One, Hugh Fraser, a Conservative member, conducted his own campaign from his house in London and some Labour MPs like Michael Barnes and Frank Allaun were instrumental in trying to get more attention and debate in the Commons.

In the early days of the war the lobby members scoured the papers for information, but a censorship of oblivion seemed to exist, so that those anxious for news looked for *Le Monde* and the *Irish Times*. As the war continued there was much more publicity both in the Press and on television and the radio. Eventually some journalists went into Biafra, though few to both sides. Fairly early on, however, the *Daily Sketch* sent a journalist and photographer and highlighted the problem. On the Continent people were amazed by the British attitude, which was to be a cause of disappointment to the staunch left-wing supporters in the lobby who had expected more concern. But within a year of the war beginning, television and radio kept the issue very much to the fore. Individuals with experience of journalism or political public relations were able to advise the lobby members and give them information.

To understand the attitude of the Left with which the lobby had to contend it is necessary to examine it in more detail. The British Left had hoped that Nigeria would prove a model democracy. This failure was sharpened by the Civil War, and the Left found it hard to forgive Biafra for this. The fact that the Portuguese were friendly towards Biafra led some to infer that the Biafrans were therefore fascist. Some supporters of the Biafra cause pointed out that Biafra was a country run by Africans and not a client state of Britain and Russia. Richard West, in an article in the *Spectator* (16 May 1969), wrote 'The Marcusist or New Left has ignored West Africa in favour of more urgent campaigns such as the demolition of capitalism or the blockade of food into the London School of Economics.' He points out that there was little difference on either side as far as capitalism went, except that Nigeria was in fact favoured by large business concerns, consortiums dealing with oil, soap and cocoa. 'If the Biafrans had been black and the Nigerians had been white, the rights and wrongs would have been much clearer. But how could the Left take sides in a war between Africans? In fact, black versus black does not evoke the emotive reaction which white versus black or black versus white does.

The Biafran Government used a Swiss public relations firm which was successful in reaching many (including all MPs) with information, but much of it was propaganda and caused irritation to a large number, who threw it into waste paper baskets. A wire service might have been more effective; though, judging by the comments made by Harold Wilson in his personal record of his years in the last Labour Government, he and his colleagues were very aware and saddened by the vast publicity given to the war and were very conscious of the strong feelings many had, even though they considered that the comments made by the supporters of Biafra were slanted unfairly against Britain. Within the Biafra lobby it was always difficult for the members to be well-informed throughout the war of the real facts within Biafra. The most effective groups were the committee chaired by Lord Brockway and the group of civil servants and others who had worked in

Eastern Nigeria who wrote a memorandum which reached Harold Wilson and other politicians and top civil servants. The Brockway Committee was not strictly part of the lobby, as it included both hawks and doves. It was an attempt to draw together those with concern on both sides who were also interested in bringing an end to the civil war.

The lobby by the civil servants, which also included some university and church people, acted in mid-1968 as a catalyst for the debates in the House of Commons, but by the end of 1968 its usefulness was possibly at an end. A skilfully drafted and well-informed memorandum was signed by thirty-eight people including a former Governor of the Eastern Region of Nigeria, all people respected in their own right as having valid experience and opinions about the situation. Copies were sent to all Members of Parliament and to the Prime Minister and many others. It was an impressive document giving an historical background to the situation and describing the different ethnic groups. Information of this kind could not be entirely ignored, and some of those who signed went back to Nigeria to do relief work and their subsequent letters helped to give accurate and up-to-date information. The memorandum was followed up a year later by a letter with five pages of signatures sent to the Prime Minister and all MPs and Bishops.

The Churches were in a difficult position because various missionary societies had missionaries in different parts of Nigeria and therefore, although they were very involved, they could not become partisan. Churches supporting work in West Africa, however, were asked to petition the Government to change its arms policy; and this was one concern, apart from relief supplies, about which the Churches did constantly urge the Government to think again. The Roman Catholic Church throughout was alive to the problems of the war and concerned with relief work. The World Council of Churches played a prominent role in relief work too. The information the missionaries were able to give to the Press about the situation of the refugees, food supplies and sickness was obviously helpful in getting continued support. Much concern was shown in Northern Ireland and Eire; undoubtedly this was because of the interest shown by the Roman Catholic Church and relief agencies, and probably also because the people in Ireland may have been more ready to question the wisdom of the British Government than many others.

The phrase 'Gowon is a Christian Gentleman' was often used

throughout the war about Nigeria's leader and undoubtedly many did trust General Gowon and thought he was making sincere efforts. This may have stopped some Church members enquiring further about the political questions involved. General Ojukwu was often photographed with beard and casual battle dress, and appeared to be unco-operative over the entry of food supplies into Biafra.

The mass of letters and telegrams that are sent when pressure groups are active have been proved effective in getting the attention of politicians. The number sent is important, for the impact of many is obvious provided the letters are genuine. They become counter-productive, however, when they are merely letters attacking in such a way that civil servants are forced into defending a policy. Letters drawing attention to a situation, or with constructive suggestions, are likely to be more effective than the purely critical ones which men in public office receive.

Some identified the Biafran Ibos with the Jews and therefore felt sympathy for them—they were becoming refugees and were herded into camps with small food supplies—yet these sympathisers were reluctant to take political action. Indeed, many Biafrans did not join the different groups in the lobby, though they had their own groups. Some had such strong feelings of distrust and disappointment in the British Government that they were not motivated to join any group, though a few did. Those with Nigerian passports were in a dilemma, for they were able to stay in Britain but knew that their reception in Nigeria would not be hospitable.

Pacifists and experienced protestors found themselves working in a group with those for whom this was their first experience of publicly organised protest. Humanists were surprised to find themselves happily engaged in speaking in Roman Catholic church halls. The marches and meetings were orderly affairs which received slight attention in the Press, perhaps due to their behaviour, and were mainly confined to Downing Street or Trafalgar Square.

The group within the lobby that specialised most in publication was the Britain Biafra Association, and although they were very active in other ways throughout the war, their consistent contribution was in publicising the facts. They were a continuously hard-working group which greatly helped the lobby's work.

The Save Biafra group was less structured and specialised in demonstration, and was avoided by the more cautious. They arranged for groups to stand outside the entrance to Downing Street at one stage in order to protest to Cabinet Ministers and civil servants who were at their place of work, instead of doing so at the weekend when they were not there. One incident they organised which was both chilling and rebuking was calling out 'Remember Biafran Dead' at the end of the one-minute silence in the Remembrance Sunday service at the Cenotaph in Whitehall.

The Friends of Biafra started successfully by sending a group to Scandinavia which succeeded in getting interest there that was sustained, but in Britain the group was not very effective throughout.

The Biafrans organised themselves into one Union and they met in smaller unions of their own townspeople too. They often held dances, where some money was raised, but also found comfort in simply meeting each other and exchanging news.

The hard core of the lobby consistently saw the issue in political terms and not just as a humanitarian fund-raising one. Some worked hard at trying to get the Labour party more concerned by attending the Labour Party Conference and distributing literature.

There were groups in other cities besides London and the Britain Biafra Association had a number of branches. One example of a group that sprang up locally was the Harringay Action Group for Peace in Nigeria. Despite its non-aggressive title it was a pro-Biafra group that was locally based and grew out of a local Church which had connections with missionaries who had served in Eastern Nigeria. People of many political persuasions were to be found in the group. The Conservative MP Hugh Rossi took an interest. On Saturdays a table was put outside the Town Hall and Turnpike Lane tube station and a petition which was already being circulated widely—'No Arms to Nigeria'—was used to gain signatures and interest. A meeting was held in the Town Hall, due to the interest of the Liberal Candidate and the Young Liberals. Some Caribbean organisations sent representatives to the meeting, and one was attended by the Labour Candidate.

Many people who did not see the issue as a political one put their energies into fund raising. The All Hallows Biafra Committee worked hard in this way, and Biafra '69 was started by a group in Chelsea who tried to raise funds by large scale fund-raising activities. A Hornchurch butcher's wife ran her own local campaign to collect food supplies, and the film star Michael Caine had his own campaign for sending a boat-load of food.

The international concern probably helped the situation at the end of the war when many more people might have been killed in revenge by the Federal forces. The power of public sympathy for Biafra by the end of the war assisted those elements in the Federal Government who were for restraint and the rebuilding of life between the war-torn parts. Considering this is the crucial problem after any civil war, Nigeria has been remarkably free from people seeking revenge.

Ironically, when the Biafran Government was finally collapsing, different groups lobbied at Westminster for immediate relief supplies to be sent, united at the end—but too late.

Ultimately the Biafra lobby failed in its political purpose to change the attitude of the British Government, but by publicly raising the affair and forcing debate they alerted the public, which was then kept informed by the mass media until the end of the war. Nigerian affairs would merit concern if only because Nigeria had been a member of the Commonwealth. The fact that she is a country on the coast of Africa greatly facilitated communication.

There are some international situations of suffering about which little is known in Britain (for example the Sudan) but in the Biafra situation there was undoubtedly enormous public sympathy aroused by the sight of starving children appearing nightly on the television screen. The humanitarian aspect of the tragedy struck home. It was a good thing that despite this mass coverage people were not anaesthetised to the suffering, but expressed their concern, if only by donations of money. Despite the slight chance of a pressure group like the Biafra lobby being able to persuade a government to reverse its policy, it would have been frightening if no one had tried to mobilise opinion in the ways which the various groups making up the lobby devised, even though in the last resort they failed.

# CUBLINGTON AIRPORT JOHN FLEWIN

There is more than one thing which can be said to be unique about the pressure group that took as its cause the campaign to keep London's Third Airport away from Cublington in North Buckinghamshire. Not least of these was that the campaign itself got more newspaper space and radio and television time than, perhaps, any other similar topic ever. But this in itself was not what was most unusual about the campaign. That, without a doubt, was the group of people who led it.

To visualise a pressure group ideal in make-up would be difficult. But anyone's picture could include some of the people who led the Cublington campaign: a newspaper chief's wife, a marketing director, an advertising executive. But would it also include two barristers, two solicitors, a farmer, a village school teacher, a market town jeweller, a trade union official, a stockbroker, a magistrate and a merchant banker? Probably it would not. But these are the people who joined together to form the Executive Committee of Wing Airport Resistance Association—WARA for short.

Two and a half years later, the activities of the people who made up this committee were described in an article in *The Times* as being 'almost disturbingly professional'. The reply to this is perhaps best summed up in the words of the Association Chairman, barrister Desmond Fennell, who answered the critics: 'They find it difficult to believe that when a group of intelligent people get together to one purpose—one that affects their own way of life—they can become as professional as, if not more professional than, the professionals in that field'. That, with the help of thousands of people whose homes and ways of life were threatened by the airport plan, is just what happened at Cublington.

It is certainly obvious from the make-up of the Committee that it was not formed as a pressure group. It was formed to wage what was almost a legal battle before the Roskill Commission. That Commission, under Mr Justice Roskill, a High Court Judge, was set up by the Labour Government to inquire into the timing and the need for a four-runway third London airport—and to find the right place to site it. Following the Stansted fiasco, Whitehall was eager to get an unchallengable choice for the site—almost a judicial choice. And the validity of that final choice by the Commission was the biggest single hurdle the Cublington campaigners had to overcome. It was almost like trying to challenge a decision taken after a High Court sitting lasting two and a half years and costing one and a half million—an awesome prospect.

Two years of the Cublington campaigners' work was taken up in the legal and technical arguments through the various stages of the Roskill procedure. Public opinion and press activity took very much of a back seat in the minds of the campaigners during this time. This back seat was available because, in announcing its short-list of four possible sites for the airport, the Commission had avoided the outcry which would have been bound to follow if an inland airport site had been stipulated immediately. The short-list included Foulness, a site on the Essex coast. Already, Foulness was the national favourite. It was seen as the answer to a lot of problems: there would be less noise over homes and towns; it was based in an area that would be affected less by huge urban developments (in fact, some quarters claimed that mass urbanisation and industrialisation of that part of Britain with its poor employment situation would be a way of solving a great many problems); it could be combined with a deep-water sea port, and so on. The advantages of Foulness were said to be unending.

However, to return to the work of the newly-formed Executive Committee. It had one aim and set out to achieve it on two fronts. The Committee's first working meeting came up with an overall objective: 'to create a climate of opinion that would make it impossible for any Government to approve the selection of an inland site for the third London airport'. The first way of attempting to achieve this was to gather together enough facts and figures to present to the Roskill Commission to prove this point. But, because of the Committee's necessary loyalty to its association's members and helpers, this had to be based on a double-sided aim: no airport at an inland site; but, if it must be inland, then it should not be at Cublington. The second front was on the Association's home ground—to raise money and recruit members. To achieve these objectives, two groups were set up within the main executive committee. To an outsider, it may have seemed an odd choice, but the person selected to lead what can only be called the local Public Relations Committee was the farmer-member, 66-year-old Bill Manning. But his family had farmed in the area for more than a century and he was highly regarded among his vast circle of friends, many of them very influential in their own fields. The legal mind of Association Chairman, barrister Fennell, went to work at the head of the other group—known, for want of a better title, as the London Committee.

Things moved quickly. The Executive Committee agreed on a target figure of £50,000; one of Britain's top barristers, formerly Secretary of State at the Ministry of Housing and Local Government, Mr Niall MacDermott QC, was appointed to present the WARA case before the Commission; MPs in the area, as far afield from Cublington as possible, were invited to become Vice Presidents. Most MPs accepted the invitation; and the Association was beginning to stock-pile its ammunition. Even at this early stage, the Committee realised that eventually the decision on the siting of the airport would have to be a parliamentary one and that as much strength as possible should be mustered on that front. Shortly afterwards a general meeting was called with a view to getting a mandate from as many people as possible in the affected area. This proved to be the real spring-board for the early campaign, although membership and fund-raising were already well under way.

In the first months of the campaign, the Committee adopted the job of educating people in the area which would be affected by the airport of the real dangers and consequences of allowing things to go ahead unchallenged. A panel of some 20 speakers were appointed and briefed. Then each of them was sent out—some nightly—to meetings in towns and villages, all of which drew packed audiences. At the same time, the local and the regional Press were being used to full advantage. They were being told of every meeting within their areas and nine times out of ten a report followed in the next editions. This flow of information to the Press was backed up by regular press hand-outs detailing how the campaign was going, how much money had been raised and was still needed and, in fact, every newsworthy point that could be put across. There were more than 30 local weekly and regional evening newspapers plus, later, one local radio station and a number of regional radio and television news programmes which were in constant use. These were *all* invaluable as they took the campaign right into people's homes, where they could not miss what was happening.

The job of collating the whole of the operation was dovetailed into a two-room office, set up in the offices of Association Secretary John Pargeter, a local solicitor. One full-time paid secretary-assistant was kept hard at work, backed up by a number of volunteers. The campaign leaders were very proud of the way the office worked and the job it did. It produced thousands of regular news-letters, plus information sheets, pamphlets and booklets which were circulated as widely as possible. Perhaps the proudest of their claims was that every member of the Association and everyone in the affected area knew almost as much about what was going on as the campaigners themselves. They considered their members had a right to be as educated in what was going on as the campaign leaders.

But, to be brief, the Committee saw its way through the various stages of Roskill in a way with which none of the members could argue. Not one of the 60,000-plus members who had been enlisted within the first few months (when the job of taking names and addresses was discontinued because of its size) could have been dissatisfied. In fact, senior members of the Roskill Commission later insisted (privately) that all that could have been done to save Cublington through the inquiry stages had been done. But it was not enough. Cublington was selected by the Commission—and so began the battle royal.

The spring-board for this campaign had been building up for some time. Aware that things might not be going according to plan, the Executive Committee had been making behind-the-scenes arrangements. But when the bombshell came it brought with it another surprise—the strength of the news media support and the public outcry that accompanied it. It was beyond the wildest of dreams of any of the Committee. The members got 24 hours warning of the decision, and within an hour of that reaching Chairman Fennell, an emergency meeting of the London Committee was called at the offices of the public relations consultants who had been retained to advise and help the campaign. The talking went on until midnight; then a number of members adjourned to meet MPs and to get parliamentary action proper under way. The seeds that had already been sown at Westminster were beginning to show their harvest. The size of the specially set-up committee in the Commons was growing day by day and reached more than 200 later on. Their expressed aim was to stop any major inland airports developments.

The rest is history, but is worth delving a little more deeply into. Perhaps the biggest stroke of luck was that the whole of public opinion at the time was on what can best be described as a crest of an environmental wave. The year that was just finish-ing—1970—had been European Conservation Year. The Govern-ment had not long beforehand set up a Department for the

Environment. And the Prime Minister had just said: 'The protection of our countryside, the avoidance of pollution, and the striking of a right balance between the needs of conservation and development are now among the most important and most difficult tasks of the Government'.

Very much alive to this mood of the country, nearly every national newspaper slammed the story of the choice of Cublington into headlines. The campaigners were, perhaps, lucky that there was no other major news story to take away the limelight. But more was to come. The second day of the battle proper was a Saturday, not the best of days to grab more headlines. But in the villages around Cublington, an underground movement—a sort of secret 'Dad's Army'—had sprung up. And whether they had planned it as such or not, they came up with what was to prove a publicity marvel for the official resistance association. They circulated in the villages a copy of a leaflet setting out how people should defend their homes in case of attack. The leaflets even went as far as to detail how to make petrol bombs. That did the trick, even though it was condemned by campaign leaders. There were front-page headlines in most Sunday newspapers talking about the villages which had declared war on Whitehall planners. Day three was easy. Sundays are normally slack news days, and picking up the threads of Saturday and Sunday newspaper stories, front pages featured the Cublington story again—and backed it up with news of the first of a series of events planned by villagers. It was something which really caught the imagination of the Press and television: the lighting of bonfires on hilltops in north Buckinghamshire and surrounding counties. This was a leaf taken from the history books—a repeat of the bonfires which warned of the Armada.

But things were moving on other fronts. Desmond Fennell and his London Committee knew that time spent on the home front was time wasted. Every effort was being directed to the one arena left open to them: Westminster. Twice Chairman Fennell went to the House of Commons to address members of the Anti-Inland Airports Committee. At that time, more than any other, the value of having a barrister at the head of the organisation was showing its benefits. Anyone else could have been inadequate for the job. He was not.

On the home front, however, the battle was nowhere near over. Two weeks after the decision, the local campaigners came up with the first of their two masterpieces. Somewhat remarkably in the middle of winter, they turned out hundreds of agricultural and industrial vehicles to form a huge procession through the threatened villages. It took a whole Sunday to get the proceedings over—but again provided the Press, radio and television with excellent Sunday material. A week later, the performance was repeated. This time it was a mass rally, held on local ground to ensure a good turn-out. That rally itself was perhaps the high point of the campaign on home territory. An estimated ten thousand people turned up on a fine afternoon and the police estimated that another two thousand were unable to get to the venue because of the huge traffic jams and miles of roads littered with parked and abandoned vehicles. It was one way in which the WARA Committee had to show Westminster and the remainder of the country how strong was their support and the weight behind their arguments. At the same time it provided a tremendous morale-booster for local people, who needed to do something to help in what were really the black days of the national campaign—when things seemed to be going the wrong way in the right places.

At about the same time, however, it began to become clear that the campaign had become more than just a battle to save 7500 acres of rural Buckinghamshire. It had become a national symbol of countryside protection—of the protection of the quality of British life. The people of Cublington had become the first people in Britain to get up and say a loud and firm 'No' to the march of concrete and development planned purely for economic considerations. For this latter question—that of economics—was the main hallmark of the campaign to discredit Roskill and, indeed, the approach to the problem in a general sense. Earlier in the Roskill proceedings, the policy of putting a value on everything, from a passenger's journey time to an historic village church, was challenged—unsuccessfully. It even came to the point of arguing about the financial value of a summer's day. Now these arguments about economics and others, both old and new, were used once again as the case against the Roskill findings came out into the open. To this end, the campaigners were helped by the eminent planning expert Professor Colin Buchanan. He was the only member of the Commission who refused to back their findings and decision. In fact, he went much further. He stated that the choice of Cublington or, for that matter, any inland site for the third London airport, would be nothing short of an environmental disaster. This was altogether the first part of the battle of words aimed at dismissing the Commission's work and taking the matter right back to stage one. The first cracks in Roskill's case were opening, and opening wide.

Soon afterwards, the Executive Committee published its own criticism of the report. All the old and many new facts and figures were presented on paper and there was just one conclusion: Foulness. Copies were sent to every MP—despite the postal strike—and every national newspaper received copies, making full use of them. There were also 1000 copies ready to go to every member of the House of Lords. But they never reached their targets: the postal strike decided that. Hand deliveries are banned in the Lords.

At about the same time, a move was made on home ground for the people living in the threatened area to take part personally in the action at Westminster. Coaches carried more than 500 women and children from the villages to the House of Commons, where they set about lobbying their own and other MPs. There was no hysteria, no banner waving, no shouting—just a quiet walk into the House, armed with words, facts and figures. What was perhaps most surprising about this excursion was that it got hardly any publicity. Certainly it got 45 seconds on the BBC's national news and a few inches in the local Press, but that was about it.

It is interesting, at this stage, to return to the early references to the actual make-up of the Association's Executive Committee and to go into a little more detail about what some of them were doing at this time. The barrister Chairman, ably assisted by the two solicitors and the stockbroker, were concentrating their efforts at Westminster, where they were meeting and talking to people as much as possible. At the same time, it was they who were drawing up the written reports, speaking to the right people, and talking on radio and television interviews. The farmer Vice-Chairman, with his own self-recruited squad of helpers from the villages in and around the airport site, was leading the home front action, assisted by the school teacher, the jeweller, the car worker and the trade union official. They were still raising money to back the London campaign. Their plans ranged from everyday village fund-raising activities like whist drives, women's soccer matches and bingo sessions to inter-village pancake races and 'It's a Knockout' competitions. These were important, and not only for fund raising: for every event kept people in the area occupied, knowing they were helping the campaign. It was, after all, really a campaign for them and they had to believe they were playing an important part in it—which they were.

Take, for example, the school teacher Committee member: Geoffrey Ginn. He was also chairman of the committee set up in his own village of Stewkley, the biggest single community that would have been wiped out by the airport. There were, as it has been said, a large number of these committees. And each one was as important as the next. But the committee at Stewkley did perhaps more than any other to back up the work being done by the WARA leadership. They were aiming at—and getting—an immense amount of national publicity. They had a rare church in their midst that was valued in money terms twice during the Roskill proceedings—once at £15,000 (the fire insurance value) and the other at five million pounds.

They dreamed up one event which was and still is almost unparalleled in such circumstances. They threw open their village and asked people from all over Britain to 'come and see what would be destroyed—our village, our homes, our country-side—and our way of life'. As it happened, there was not as much pre-publicity as could have been hoped for. But it worked. Thousands of people flocked to Stewkley and surrounding villages to find out what it was all about—and sip free tea in villagers' homes. This move did as much as any to put over to the country at large what the whole thing was about—and engendered a huge amount of goodwill not only among the visitors, but through the after-publicity that the event got.

But the Stewkley Committee, under the leadership of headmaster Ginn, were not content to leave it there. They made personal contact with nearly every MP. They reproduced—as it happened, without permission—in a wonderfully presented booklet the report of Professor Buchanan opposing the majority verdict of the Roskill Commission. Each copy was individually printed with each MP's name and constituency on the cover. It was something which could not have escaped notice, even in an MP's busy office. At the same time as all this activity and financing their own part of the campaign, the people of Stewkley raised thousands of pounds for the main WARA fighting fund.

To return to the original subject. If the campaigners of Cublington are to be described as a pressure group, they were 100,000 members strong by this time—enough, really, to win a minor war. And that was just the way in which they set about tackling the emergency of the airport plan.

Within the immediate area of the proposed airport site, the whole thing was treated something like a major emergency.

Nearly everyone made full use of all their talents—and some of them talents they didn't know they possessed. Certainly, it was not what would normally be envisaged when the words 'pressure group' are mentioned. It certainly was not, however, the high-powered, expert and master-minded public relations exercise that it has been branded. If it was professionally handled, it was for the reasons already stated: that the leaders of the campaign were ordinary but intelligent people who took on one purpose and used everything they knew to pull off victory. In fact, if proof were needed of these statements, it could be found in the Association's final balance sheet. Money raised: £57,810; legal and administration costs: £47,896; and publicity: £9,344. This final figure is hardly enough to pay for a two-month long high-pressure selling campaign, let alone one that lasted for two and a half years.

When the Minister of Technology, Mr John Davies, stood up in the Commons on 26 April 1971 to announce that the Government had decided that Foulness was the right place for the new airport, it was not the conclusion of 'an almost disturbingly professional' campaign. It was a victory for democracy—for people who used the democratic system to its fullest.

# THE DISABLEMENT INCOME GROUP
### BRIAN FROST

'Let's have a standard for human kindness'—'Her battle is for the needy disabled'—'Test poll on behalf of the wheelchair group'—'Do you "Dig" DIG ?'—these are typical of the headlines filling the pages of the British Press in recent years. Hardly any paper, whether the *Guardian,* the *Daily Telegraph,* the *Evening Standard* or *The Times*, failed to draw its readers' attention to one of Britain's most successful and imaginative pressure groups. Indeed, the Disablement Income Group has been adept at getting itself into the newspapers pictorially as well as editorially. When mass readership papers like the *Daily Express,* the *Sun* and the *Daily Mirror* give photographic cover, then a pressure group knows it is reaching millions of people and influencing them.

What made this pressure group hard news ? *Tribune,* the left-wing newspaper, pin-pointed its efficacy when it reported a demonstration in 1967. 'There was another demonstration in Trafalgar Square last Sunday afternoon', it wrote. 'But this was a different kind of organisation. Most people came not by bus or tube but in wheelchairs and ambulances. And when it was over, 150 of them went down Whitehall to Downing Street. Despite the organiser's efforts many were there who ought not to have come. For a man or a woman with polio or multiple sclerosis to come all the way from Liverpool or Rotherham to London is a dangerous and desperate thing. But the disabled are *becoming* desperate.'

To get Press coverage of this kind is one thing. Much hard work must have gone into mobilising such an effective visual presence in Trafalgar Square that Sunday. All pressure groups which succeed do so because of the interaction of ideas, personalities, timing, and the efficacy with which they are advocates of their cause. DIG was no exception; it was effective in its early days because of the driving power and the determination of Megan Du Boisson, herself the victim of multiple sclerosis.

It had all started with a letter to the Press in which she and a friend had asked people to write to her if they were interested in putting pressure where it mattered to make sure that the needs of the disabled—for whatever reason—were met more adequately. This letter about pensions for the disabled appeared in the *Guardian,* 22 March 1965:

'Common sense informed the whole of Mary Stott's article (March 15th) in which she outlined the existing pockets of need and distress which the Welfare State appears to ignore; perhaps even to encourage by its insistence on the existing rules and regulations.

But we should like to talk about a particular aspect of her article: the need for provision of a disability pension for all who are disabled, the amount being in proportion to the degree of disablement. This need is more readily admitted in the case of an earning member of the family, but when the mother of the family, whose main care is the home, finds herself unable to run her home without a considerable amount of help, incurring great additional expense, then few people would support the idea of a pension for her, it seems.

And yet those who dissent would readily agree to the children being taken into care (at great cost to the community) while the disabled woman is taken into a 'home' and the husband tries to live on his own, visiting the children and his wife. The cost of this in terms of suffering for all the members of the family is incalculable and we admire with all our mind and heart the work of Ann Armstrong in this connection.

A recent article in your columns on the 'chronic sick' was relevant to this, for sometimes almost a lifetime can be spent in institutions, and with the expenditure of thought and the money which would otherwise be given to hospitalising the invalid it would be possible to keep families together. We would suggest the foundation of a group, to which all societies, such as those for people with muscular dystrophy, multiple sclerosis, poliomyelitis, and other long term diseases would contribute their ideas and authority.

This group could be called the Disablement Income Group or DIG. It would exist only to correlate the work of the other groups in regard solely to getting recognition for the *right* of disabled persons irrespective of the reason for that disablement, to pensions from the State to enable them to live in a reasonable degree of independence and dignity *in their own homes*.

The principle of this idea is accepted and acted upon in other countries in Europe, such as Norway and Sweden; and possibly in others as well. At this point we declare our interest: we both have multiple sclerosis. But, taking up Mary Stott's challenge because 'someone has to do it', we invite any person or society interested to write to us about DIG—the Disablement Income Group.

Yours faithfully

Megan du Boisson and Berit Moore,
Rellan House, Busbridge Lane, Godalming, Surrey.

As a result of this, letters began to pour in from disabled people which revealed an appalling situation of need. Megan Du Boisson was married and had enough money. What would be happening to her if there was not enough money to pay for the extra things she needed and to allow her to be a good mother and wife as she tried to use her disability creatively? The letters gave the answer: there was pain, suffering, victimisation. The one and a half million people suffering from permanent disability were on the touch-lines of British society. Unlike other countries in Europe, Norway in particular, little had yet been done in the British Isles.

But something *was* done as a result of this letter to the *Guardian.* Mrs Du Boisson drew a group of people round her who had shrewdness, devotion and loyalty. Though there were times when it was not clear if this new pressure group would survive, both Mrs Du Boisson and her supporters turned out to be born crusaders and by their hard work, courage and belief in what they were doing they managed to persuade others that action had to be taken at a governmental level.

At that time Douglas Houghton was preparing a review of the social services for the Labour Administration and the Labour Party itself was hammering out its policy. The Disablement Income Group was asked to submit information and give advice. It had access to the corridors of power. Many pressure groups wish for this but they are not always successful in being listened to by those in power. DIG was respected at a government level because it did its homework, knew its facts and was accurate. Moreover, it had specific, concrete, attainable aims—it knew it wanted to alter the statute books and in what direction. Its aims were as follows: to secure for all disabled people a national disability income and an allowance for the extra expense of disablement; to co-operate with other bodies working in the field for the improvement of the economic and social position of disabled people and the chronic sick; and to promote research into the economic and social problems of disablement.

DIG was of course fortunate in having clear goals. It was fortunate, too, that in terms of the party political conflicts in Britain disablement was a cross-party issue. Even though DIG was a pressure group, and as such unable to receive money for its pressure group work (although its educational work receives 'charitable status') it had the support of a large number of Members of Parliament, including an All-Party Committee on Disablement. Because of this—and the fact that in a sense its growth and timing coincided with a change in the national awareness of the problems of the disabled—its achievement has been considerable. On 19 January 1970, in the course of the Second Reading of the National Superannuation and Social Insurance Bill, the Secretary of State for the Social Services, then Mr. Richard Crossman, said:

> ...I should like to refer to clause 17... the only new provision... which provides for a constant attendance allowance. I should like to say this personally. There has been a growing demand, of which that remarkable organisation the Disablement Income Group has been the spearhead, for special provision for over and above what is already given for anyone seriously handicapped on disablement. We have all been deeply moved by the lives as well as the words of people like Anne Armstrong and Megan Du Boisson. Without them it may well be that clause 17 would never have found its place in the Bill.'
>
> (Hansard report)

Mr. Crossman was not the only person to witness to the power of DIG. During the passage of the National Insurance (Old Persons' and Widows' Pensions and Attendance Allowance) Act of 23 July 1970, the then Secretary of State Sir Keith Joseph had this to say:

> 'Lastly, I come perhaps to the most important innovation of all, the first step in a better treatment for the disabled. This was common ground between the parties, though the credit has to be given to the Labour Party for starting upon legislation. As a long-standing supporter of DIG and of other similar bodies, I should like to pay tribute to Mrs Armstrong of the Responaut and to that astonishing woman, the late Mrs Megan Du Boisson of the DIG, for drawing so vividly to public attention the plight of the disabled. It was a remarkable tragedy for this country that in one month last year, through accident in one case and a lingering death in another, the community lost Mrs Du Boisson, the leading figure in DIG, and The Revd Mary Webster, the founder and leader of the National Council for the Single Woman and her Dependents, which work for women who often give up their lives to care for disabled parents. We are starting now on the process of a period of better treatment of the disabled and the Bill is the first step at which both Mrs Megan Du Boisson and The Revd Mary Webster would have rejoiced.'
>
> (Hansard report)

It was a tribute to Mrs Du Boisson's flair for creating and

sustaining an organisation that it went from strength to strength after her tragic death in a car crash. She had been a person who made a dynamic impression on all with whom she came into contact, but she had been careful not to rely only on the strength of her personality. She had built up round her people with many gifts, some of them disabled, others not, who carried on what she had started, determined to make legislation the key to the alleviation of the many problems suffered by disabled people.

What did the legislation achieve? By the end of 1971 through this Act (and a Private Member's Bill: The Chronically Sick and Disabled Persons Act, 1970) around 50,000 individuals who satisfy the Attendance Allowance Board of their need for attendance by some other person day and night receive an attendance allowance of £4 a week. This involves payment of £10 million a year (less than half of one per cent of the total outlay on Social Security benefits, in fact) to the most severely disabled people, who receive this money not as a charity but as their inalienable right as citizens.

Put technically, the two milestones of 1970 state that an Attendance Allowance be introduced from 6 December 1971 for all very severely disabled people at home who satisfy the Attendance Allowance Board of their need for attendance by some other person day and night. The allowance will be for the flat rate of £4 a week free of tax, without means test or contributions qualifications. Local authority services and facilities for disabled people, previously permissive, are now mandatory. The aim of this legislation is to bring the poorest authority services up to the standard of the best.

Much hard work had been done to make people aware of the minority group of disabled people. DIG brilliantly points the way to handle the type of problem increasingly obvious in a large, bureaucratic society. They are what might be termed 'half-way' problems. There are some issues too big to be dealt with by individuals, or small groups, yet not so massive as to push themselves to the forefront of domestic politics. For their alleviation they need a well organised, clearly informed pressure group before effective change can be seen.

How did the Disablement Income Group go about its work and gain such respect? Apart from a quite systematic attempt at publicity it produced well documented material for professional people involved in the world of the social services. It also produced material for the disabled themselves to help them understand their rights. Many people give up in despair in the face of the strange anomalies of the Welfare State, and part of DIG's work was to present complex legislation in such a way as to be readily intelligible.

At a national level it produced a book on the comparative treatment of disability in Europe (*Social Security and Disability*), which influenced politicians at the top of the main British Political parties. It kept before the general public the fact of disability in programmes on the mass media and in the newspapers. 'The Price of Pain' (BBC 'Money Programme') and the ITV 'Report' in November 1970 were useful means of reaching a wide audience. Other programmes which included the work of the group were 'World at One' and a reading of the poetry of Mrs Du Boisson. For internal consumption the group produced a quarterly bulletin and a number of specialist papers like Jane Outram's 'Right to help?' illustrating the inadequacies of Supplementary Benefit in dealing with cases of hardship due to disability.

In addition, a network of groups was built up throughout Britain. Membership in 1970 was about 6500, mostly disabled. 5000 of these belonged to one or other local branch and 1300 were individual members. A successful local branch, as the Press cuttings at the Group's headquarters show, can get a number of news items into the local newspaper and often influence an MP by inviting him or her to a specific event, or by presenting a petition worked out as part of a nation-wide campaign stemming from a carefully worked out policy.

When assessing the work of DIG, however, questions have to be asked about its next stage; for its first task is over. The freshness and novelty of its approach, intimately connected with the charismatic personality of its founder, has lost its original impact. There has been a certain amount of parliamentary legislation. Many have been helped to cope with their disability more effectively. It has been possible for them to talk through their problems and gain a certain self-dignity. Mary Greaves, herself disabled, and one of the successors to Mrs Du Boisson, was invited by Sir Keith Joseph to become the Attendance Allowance Board's first lay member. Even the then Prime Minister, Mr Edward Heath, recognised the influence of the pressure group's work. When presented with the results of its European study project by Miss Mary Greaves he remarked: 'Very largely due to the work of the Disablement Income Group the problems and hardships of disabled people have been brought to the fore and to the attention of Parliament in the last few years. I recognise that such work needs to be done and I welcome the advice and co-operation which you are able to give my colleagues most closely concerned.'

But, although the first task is over, maybe only half the battle has been won. The actual amount of money allowed is small, as the cost of living continues to rise. Much remains to be done, and in 1970 DIG saw its role in this way:

> 'The definition and the assessment of disability raise formidable problems. DIG is campaigning for every type of disability, which for our purposes may be defined as a physical, mental or sensory handicap, medically ascertainable, which causes a long-term reduction in working capacity and/or a significant increase in living expenses. In the past year we have been able to clarify our proposals for meeting these two consequences. Detailed medical assessments, similar to those used for industrial injury, seem neither practicable nor appropriate since we are not seeking compensation for loss of faculty. What we do seek is parity of treatment on a common basis of need so that financial benefit for all who are seriously disabled is assured in relation to that need and is not confined to an inadequate and irrelevant temporary sickness benefit or to a system of supplementary benefit devised as emergency help to the able-bodied people. But as well as providing specifically for the 'civilian disabled', we have got to get away from rigid adherence to an exclusive contributory principle of national insurance otherwise we shall never be able satisfactorily to provide for disabled housewives (by which we mean married women whose work is solely in the home) or for those who through disability at birth or in childhood have never been able to work.'
>
> (Quoted from DIG pamphlet, 1970)

What does DIG propose to deal with this situation? First, a National Disability Income, subject to tax, for total loss of working capacity, with a reduced rate of benefit when the loss is substantial but not total; secondly, a Disability Expense Allowance, tax-free and non-means tested, towards the extra cost of living (and/or working) with a physical, mental or sensory handicap. The full disability income would be the same as the normal retirement pension at the basic rate or graduated rate as appropriate. The Disability Expense Allowance would be extended from the new Attendence Allowance to cover a less narrow category of disabled people.

In a closely-worded pamphlet DIG has spelled out what it expects of Parliament and geared its campaign in its second—and more difficult—stage to the document which it has prepared on disability in seven West European countries. It argues that if its proposals are carried through, the following results will be obtained:

   (i) a saving in means-tested supplementary benefits;

   (ii) fewer disabled people being cared for in long-stay institutions, and fewer of their children being in the care of local authorities; and

   (iii) the increased use of working capacity of disabled people.

DIG is now at the stage where it is on the point of becoming a movement. Like the Child Poverty Action Group, perhaps its nearest neighbour in style, approach and type of parliamentary action envisaged, it has to face up to several facts: Can it sustain its impact over a number of years? Can it win its points without seeing them watered down? Can it keep money and enthusiasm flowing in its direction  For there are many pressure groups which come and go and fail in their ultimate objectives.

Few countries have worked out a way of dealing with the problems disablement brings. In Europe there are only two countries which guarantee pensions for all disabled: Denmark and Sweden. In France disabilities arising from a congenital defect or childhood disease are expressly excluded from the pension scheme. In other countries regulations concerning minimum contribution periods mean those never able to work have not been eligible to join an insurance scheme and so are not entitled to a pension. The three Scandinavian countries, however, all award pensions to the disabled housewife, though in Norway she may be debarred from the scheme by her lack of necessary contributions. The award of a pension is based on her incapacity to perform household duties, which is assessed in exactly the same way as the incapacity to engage in outside employment.

If in these countries—which have in some ways, though only marginally, altered attitudes to disablement—change has been slow, have we be wrong in attributing to DIG such influence, and may not its second phase prove ineffective when it comes to substantial rather than marginal alteration to the legislation at Westminster? I think not. DIG is a very skilled pressure group. In the first place, it is not afraid of publicity, and not afraid to provide material for various types of magazines and newspapers. One of the reporters on the *Sun* regards it as her job to enable that paper to report accurately and be interested in social problems in a positive way. But she has commented that often people with a strong social conscience spurn popular newspapers and journals. DIG never makes that mistake. One of its earliest articles appeared in *Tit-bits.*

In the second place, DIG realises that pressure groups must know their facts. It is not enough for social scientists to itemise poverty, as Michael Harrington's *The Other America* did in the 1950s, and Professor Titmuss's work on hidden pockets of misery did for Britain in the 1960s. These have to be made known and presented in places of power in an attractive, compelling manner.

In the third place, DIG has originality. It decided to bring disability out of a corner and aimed to help its victims live as active and full a life as possible. At the same time as the world poverty lobby was putting stress on the need of people in the Third World to determine their own lives—not, in effect, to have things 'done' for them by the rich part of the world—DIG articulated the psychological problems of people who were discriminated against because of their physical disability. It was quick to see the need for parables; and in an artist like Michael Flanders or a member of the House of Lords like Lady Masham, it knew it had personalities who could draw attention to the many unknown people struggling in loneliness and despair with their disablement. And parables in people such as these two presented had a dual role—to help the public to a new awareness and insight, but also to help those who were disabled to a new understanding of themselves. To us now it might seem an obvious point, yet in the early days of DIG a number of doctors expressed considerable resistance to its ideas because they thought those with disability should not be exposed to the public glare.

Fourthly, even though DIG has an immense pastoral role to perform, when it comes to effecting change it is hard-headed. Its appeal is based not only on the justice of its case (there are, after all, many causes which are manifestly just but which end in failure) but on its logic, reason and cogency. It has gained a reputation among parliamentarians and civil servants for doing its background reading. It was willing to look at the economic facts of life and 'to submit papers not sermons'.

Finally, it has a profound feel for the 'consumer': it knows its constituency well. Where the Child Poverty Action Group has been a small group of well-informed social theorists and activists, the DIG grapevine has been involved in the all too human day-to-day tragedies of disablement. At the same time as it is trying to change the attitude of officials in social security offices, it is aiming to help its clients adjust to disability in a creative way.

Is all this enough? The next ten years will show whether it is or not. Can DIG put on pressure to alter the backward way in which Britain looks at disablement? Can legislation be given priority in a House of Commons often over-burdened with Bills? Is there a real desire for radical change? It is too early to tell. But DIG's 1960s work has been well grounded for its second phase. Many know that the disablement award is meagre and that as the cost of living increases renewed efforts will have to be sustained. But a start has been made, and old-fashioned attitudes are being changed. An attempt has been made to bring justice to one part of the world which, before DIG's appearance, was lodged more in charitable work than in legislation, and more in suffering in dark, back streets than in the bright lights of Trafalgar Square.

Many local authorities are beginning to work out the implications of the legislation in Parliament, some of them in a notable way, like Canterbury in Kent. Others, like The Royal Borough of Kensington and Chelsea, have employed researchers to find how many people are still in need of help, yet not in touch with any of the available provisions. There are many like these who need to be reached, and this is a problem not only for groups like DIG but for the whole community.

The Labour Government has in 1974 appointed the first Minister to deal with disablement in the history of the world; but if this means that the needs of the disabled are to be treated as a thing apart from the rest of the community, and made too special, this might prove a backward rather than a forward step.

What progressive local authorities are now doing, in conjunction with pressure groups and concerned people within Parliament and in certain given localities, is good; but much needs to be done before we can be satisfied. The whole community must ensure that the good work started by pioneer individuals and groups is continued and developed.

# THE PRESSURE GROUP PHENOMENON
## WILLIAM WALLACE

There is nothing new about pressure group activity in Britain, and little that is new in the means of pressure open to the concerned and the interested. Many of the new organisations which have grown up during the last ten years have defended causes which were the concern of similar groups fifty or a hundred years ago, and have used methods which for all their apparent novelty would be familiar to many a nineteenth-century activist. What has changed, and is still changing, is the context of group activity: the legal rules which set the bounds of political activity, the patterns of party politics and of governmental structure within which (or occasionally outside which) groups operate, the economic and social developments which affect the opportunities available to groups and the nature of the problems with which they are concerned.

The bases for group activity as we know it developed gradually from the late eighteenth century into the nineteenth. There needed first to be an urban society, in which substantial groups of people were closely dependent on each other, in which a wide range of distinct social and economic roles had developed, and in which at least some members of society outside the ruling group had sufficient leisure from the immediate necessities of working, eating and sleeping to reflect on and be active about wider social concerns. The protestant religion, most of all in the nonconformist churches, had created a sense of social conscience and individual concern which fostered such activity, and the education which the nonconformist churches prized gave them access to books and to the critical Press. The laws of treason and of libel had been relaxed sufficiently to enable the emergence of a fairly free Press, providing news about foreign developments and government policy and a focus for informed discussion. Parliament remained sufficiently independent of governmental patronage to act as a check on the executive; with such a small and simple government machine Parliament provided the obvious channel of access for popular protest and popular appeal.

The earliest groups were necessarily led by the leisured well-to-do, concerned either to promote their own interests or to improve the lot of others. Much of their support was also limited to the same section of society, the literate and the economically independent, from the progressive 'gentleman' or clergyman to the self-employed businessman or artisan. The 'mob' in eighteenth-century London had its own means of violent direct action for political self-expression. One of the first causes to be taken up in this way was that of the abolition of the slave trade and of slavery, a long and difficult campaign pursued from small beginnings in the late eighteenth century to gradual success in suppressing first the British slave-trade, then foreign slave-traders, and then slavery in the British colonies. In this the Anti-Slavery Society was pitted against the influential and organised West Indian sugar interests, well represented in the Commons. Parliament was the Society's main target, using weapons not unfamiliar to activists today. Before the General Election of 1830 a suggested questionnaire to candidates on slavery was published, and in 1833 a petition with a million and a half signatures was presented to Parliament. Pamphlets and articles supporting the case, aimed at the interested public, were intended to affect the climate of opinion in their favour, and so to bring social pressures to bear on wavering opponents.

The nineteenth century saw a succession of causes taken up successfully by organised groups moved by self-interest or by idealism, or more often by some blend of these two: free trade, political reform, the right to 'combine' in trade unions, prison reform, better conditions of work for children and for adults in factories. Partly as a result of their improving efforts, the government which they were lobbying grew both in size and in terms of responsibilities, creating new ministries, new boards and commissions of regulation, over some of which the more 'respectable' groups exerted some considerable influence. The extension of the franchise and the growth of mass education, together with the movements for workers' education and self-improvement, brought the working classes into conventional politics, and created opportunities for mass movements and 'popular' groups. They also led to the development of the mass political party, with members and branches throughout the country and a parliamentary party which owed some part of its success to their efforts in its support. Popular education created the basis for the popular press, ever ready to uncover a new scandal or take up a new cause. The expansion of government created a civil service with a degree of independence from parliamentary scrutiny, and a need for information on movements of opinion as well as on social and economic trends. Economic growth, increasing urbanisation, and the involvement of government in social improvement and economic regulation alleviated some of the problems about which groups had agitated, and gave rise to others in their stead.

New targets for group activity thus appeared, to compete for their attention with Parliament and informed opinion. The political parties might agree to include their demands in a manifesto, or use their growing control over parliamentary time to advance or to obstruct a particular measure. Other organisations, above all the powerful combinations of employers and of workers, might agree to assist in lobbying the government on an issue, or even to take direct action by refusing to co-operate with the government in a related area or by 'blacking' related goods. The Press might take up a cause and build it up into a newspaper campaign. Government departments might prove receptive to group proposals and willing to provide information on government intentions, so that close relationships between a multitude of groups and 'their' Ministries developed.

The tactics available to groups were gradually refined and extended by the growth of government and the development of an educated and industrialised urban mass society. Where government departments had come to rely on the co-operation of groups, that co-operation could be denied or subjected to certain conditions. Mass literacy extended the potential for mass propaganda. A more centralised and interdependent economy made selective but effective disruption of economic life and communications much easier. Opportunities to gain widespread publicity from small-scale demonstrations were extended first by the popular Press and by photography, and further by the development of radio and the cinema. So group activity moved in opposite but complementary directions, away from the open process of parliamentary petitioning towards private consultation with civil servants and ministers, and towards new forms of direct action. Suffragettes chained themselves to railings, or even threw themselves under horses at race meetings. Dockers refused to load *The Jolly George* when it was bound for Poland during the Russo-Polish war.

The two World Wars of this century completed the process by which organised groups and group activity became accepted as a central part of the procedures of British government. The major economic interests, both the employers and the trade unions, were taken into partnership by a government concerned to get the most out of a war-mobilised economy, establishing rights of consultation over areas of policy which they have successfully maintained since. Voluntary services, many of them based on local non-official organisations, gave invaluable help on the 'home front'. As significantly, political dissent was not entirely suppressed during wartime; during World War II political education and political discussion were treated as part of the war effort, and groups concerned with the sort of society that peace might bring and the sort of peace which Britain ought to aim for continued to operate, and even on occasion promoted candidates in by-elections against the coalition parties.

The intending activist is therefore faced with a political system which is well accustomed to organised groups, and which to an extent depends on the interaction between different groups for its effective operation. To a greater or lesser extent all Government Departments except the Treasury, the Cabinet Office and the Civil Service Department maintain regular contacts with established groups in their area. Many of these, of course, directly represent affected interests. No Minister of Agriculture would now ignore the National Farmers' Union, no Minister of Education the various teachers' unions, no Secretary of State for Health and Social Security the British Medical Association. But many other recognised groups represent the interests of others, or promote some general cause. The close relationship between the aid lobby and the Ministry of Overseas Development has already been described. The Foreign and Commonwealth Office similarly looks to the United Nations Association for support in keeping international issues in front of ordinary people, and in return accepts its advice and its representations. The Home Office looks to the Howard League for Penal Reform for evidence of the climate of informed opinion in its field and for suggestions on future policy; and in return keeps the League informed about the evolution of policy within the ministry.

Civil servants cultivate these close relations with recognised unofficial groups not because they want in any way to circumvent the democratic process, but because their Minister and Parliament expect them to. A Minister needs information about the attitudes of people in his 'constituency', those whom his Department is responsible for assisting or controlling; he wants to generate public support for ministerial policies, and to anticipate (and if possible avoid) criticism. Civil servants are expected to be able to brief their political masters on likely sources of support and criticism, to steer them towards the one and away from the other. Politicians commonly desire to be popular, and ministerial departments, like most large organisations, to avoid trouble; both desires, in a relatively free and open political system, push them towards co-operation with organised groups.

A major source of trouble and of criticism for minister and civil servant is still the House of Commons. A well-placed Parliamentary Question can generate demands for further debate or enquiry, or catch the headlines in the next day's Press. The pace of work in some ministries is noticeably easier during the parliamentary recess, free from the 'burden' of daily criticism which Parliament focuses upon them, through questions, through debates, and through committee investigations. The thinness of the quality Press during the Christmas and Easter recesses testifies to the extent to which parliamentary activity generates news material and concentrates public attention.

In spite of recent improvements in salaries, allowances, and staffing, the British MP remains one of the least well-equipped parliamentarians in the developed world in terms of secretarial assistance and research facilities. Those MPs who do not have easy access to a party research department, or who cannot afford to pay for additional staff out of their own pocket—that is, the vast majority of them—are therefore heavily dependent on the assistance of outside groups for the provision of information, suggestions for speeches or for letters to ministers and to the Press, and even draft amendments and draft parliamentary questions. During the committee stage of a Bill the lobbyists of affected interests and concerned groups, often pitted against each other, haunt the corridors of Westminster, exchanging hurried conversations with 'their' MPs and supplying them with briefs from which to speak as they slip out of the committee room and back again. Ministers and their civil servants are well aware of this constant activity, and cultivate good relations with groups on different sides of a difficult issue in the hope of gaining advance warning, and so of minimising the embarrassment an awkward parliamentary exchange might cause. Academic writing on the 'decline' of Parliament and complaints by back-benchers about the weakness of the House of Commons in resisting ministerial dominance should not be taken as implying that Parliament is no longer worth considering a major target of pressure group activity: it remains one of the most effective means of ensuring publicity for an interest or a cause and of exerting pressure on the Government.

The political parties are also well accustomed to group pressure. In both major parties active membership of groups the aims of which do not conflict too sharply with party policy is on the whole a positive recommendation for the young man seeking a candidacy and the MP seeking office—a factor which considerably helps groups to penetrate party policy groups and Parliament. Party Conferences attract 'fringe' meetings, often very well attended, on housing, aid, social reform, and above all in recent years on the Middle Eastern question, promoted by pressure groups independent of any party. Before the 1970 Election both parties competed for the approval of some of the social reform groups, the Labour Government for instance strongly contesting the criticisms of the Child Poverty Action Group, the Conservatives promising to implement some of its demands if elected.

The news media look to groups as a significant source of material: supplying information, suggestions for articles, reports of activity or activities themselves for journalists to cover, or detailed examinations of government actions or social problems for the media to take up. So do a wide range of interested people, sufficiently aware of a problem to want to know more about it and sufficiently wary of governmental secrecy and of the mass media to want to find alternative sources of information. Any pressure group which manages to gain a modicum of publicity is therefore likely to find itself besieged with demands for literature and information, not only as with the Disablement Income Group and the Homosexual Law Reform Society from people within its natural constituency, but also from schoolteachers looking for materials for current affairs discussions and schoolchildren writing essays, from amateur debaters preparing speeches on the subject, from potential activists and from potential opponents. The popular expectation that pressure groups are a reliable and ready source of information is matched by a popular expectation that the material they ask for should be provided free of charge; but it serves to provide new groups with a further opportunity of disseminating their propaganda and hopefully promoting their cause.

The pattern of established groups in British politics is one of bewildering profusion, too varied for any easy classification. Most academic classifications distinguish between 'interest groups' and 'promotional groups'. Groups which represent and promote their own economic interests, such as the Confederation of British Industry and the Trade Union Congress, the National Federation of

Old-Age Pensioners and the British Trawlers Federation, are classified as interest groups; bodies which promote social causes or the interests of others, such as Anti-Apartheid or the Peace Pledge Union, are classified as promotional groups. But many organisations fall between these overall categories. Of the groups covered in this review, the Disablement Income Group drew much of its support from the disabled; but its success so far has depended on its ability to identify its cause with social values more general than those of economic interest alone. Wing Airport Resistance Association set out to defend the continued economic and social existence of the Cublington area, in terms which were more widely defined than local interests alone. Similarly the National Union of Teachers claims to be as concerned with the quality of education in this country as with the interests of its members, and the Association of British Chambers of Commerce as concerned with national prosperity as with its members' profitability. Some of the newer social reform groups, particularly in the housing area, have added a new dimension to this by attempting to involve those whom they are trying to help in working to improve their own conditions.

It may be useful to distinguish a few further differences between organisations within what we may accept as the loosely defined category of promotional groups. Some of the best established bodies are concerned with general issues rather than specific causes, and sponsor or assist specific campaigning groups when particular issues arise. The United Nations Association is concerned to promote support in Britain for issues which the UN considers of international importance, from aid to human rights to environmental pollution. The National Council for Civil Liberties is concerned with the whole range of libertarian issues which campaigning groups take up from time to time; the Movement for Colonial Freedom (now renamed Liberation) with the struggle for independence throughout the world. All three have fathered new specific organisations, and helped or co-operated with many others. Many other bodies only intermittently act as pressure groups. The Automobile Association or the Ramblers' Association, for instance, have many functions other than lobbying the government. Churches and trade unions are not primarily concerned with the promotion of political causes; but both have on many occasions espoused particular issues. Though in recent years union support has rarely gone further than passing motions at conferences, the churches have proved valuable allies for a number of causes, not only for the aid lobby.

Another line of differentiation may be drawn between groups with limited aims which are content to work within the established political system and groups with aims which cannot easily be met within the existing political structure. At one extreme on this spectrum lie those bodies which are recognised as responsible and authoritative by the Government Departments with which they consult, and which are consequently inhibited in their criticisms by the need to retain the confidence, and protect the confidences, of the civil servants who consult them. At the other extreme lie movements such as the Vietnam Solidarity Campaign, concerned more to affirm their cause and to assert their rejection of a system which opposes it than to compromise in the hope of making at least a little progress towards their long-term objective. In between stretch layers of connected and often overlapping organisations. For the Howard League to have campaigned openly for the abolition of capital punishment would have jeopardised its close relationship with the Home Office; so it supported the establishment of the separate National Council for the Abolition of the Death Penalty, to take up the issue in a more active campaign. The peace movement and the collection of organisations concerned to bring pressure to bear to end white rule in Southern Africa reflect in their organisational divisions the successive rejection by new generations of the compromises which new activists considered their elders to have made with the established system, and the pattern of eventual compromise which each generation has adopted in its turn.

The potential activists considering forming a promotional association will thus find the field already well occupied by established bodies, some highly considered and regularly active, others more or less moribund. He may find that some will resent the incursion of a new organisation into what they regard as 'their' field; or he may find welcome and willing allies, or a general body which welcomes affiliation and will provide advice and support. If he is concerned with a 'new' but contentious issue, his promotional group is unlikely to hold the field unopposed for long. The RAC and the AA are opposed on many issues by the Pedestrians' Association. The Abortion Law Reform Association found itself rapidly faced by the counter-organisation of the Society for the Protection of the Unborn Child. The Divorce Law Reform Union aroused the Mothers' Union, the National Board of

Catholic Women, and several other organisations to oppose its efforts.

Groups can also be distinguished by the different characteristics of their objectives. The pressure group with the best chance of achieving its aims is the organisation with a clear and limited objective which already commands some sympathy within the Government and in Parliament, and which it is within the power of the Government to grant. Conversely, a group which sets out to promote general and widely-drawn objectives, for which politicians and civil servants have little current sympathy (or about which they as yet know little), or which can only be affected to a limited degree by the actions of the British Government, must resign itself to a longer and more difficult campaign; unless it is concerned less with the gradual achievement of partial successes through the low compromises of conventional politics than with the affirmation of the righteous of its cause, and therefore abandons conventional pressure altogether for mass demonstrations or revolutionary activity. A group therefore needs to be as clear as it can be about its aims if it is to select the right targets for its efforts, and the appropriate tactics to get its message across.

For an organisation like the Wing Airport Resistance Association its aim was simple and short-term. It wanted to influence and to deflect a Government decision. If it succeeded, the organisation could happily be wound up; if it failed, there would be little point in continuing. Its targets—the Roskill Commission, MPs from affected constituencies, the Minister concerned—were therefore clear. Its arguments, moreover, already commanded a considerable degree of public sympathy from environmentalists and others outside the area likely to be affected by the airport; it needed therefore to arouse public opinion, not first to convert it.

Similarly, the Disablement Income Group could anticipate public sympathy for its objectives if public attention could successfully be caught and its case put across. Politicians do not like to appear hard-faced or unfeeling; it could therefore expect, within a climate of opinion which already expected the Government to look after disadvantaged groups, to meet at most with arguments that money or resources could not yet be found, that 'the time is not yet ripe', in opposition to its demands. Its immediate objective was straightforward, and could be concentrated into the simple packaging of a private member's bill.

More difficult problems for such groups follow the achievement of their short-term objective, in making the transition from a limited campaign to a more general concern with the welfare of those they are concerned to help. The contrast with the Homosexual Law Reform Society is worth stressing here. The latter's objective was similarly straightforward, similarly focused on a change in the law which could be accomplished through private members' legislation. But better treatment for homosexuals was not a cause which politicians were in general happy to support on public platforms, or which the popular Press would instinctively support. The ground had therefore to be prepared, by a long campaign of information and persuasion, before it became possible to hope to carry a Bill through Parliament.

The nature of Shelter's aims dictated a different style of approach, and a different set of targets. To change the Government's housing policy, to affect the way in which politicians discuss the housing problem and the allocation of the national budget, required a more general campaign to arouse the Government, Parliament and the public, to provide evidence of public committment and of popular concern. A major problem for groups like Shelter is to measure the extent of their achievement, since their aims are expressed in general terms and not attainable through government decisions or changes in the law alone. A similar problem existed for the aid lobby, in working for a cause without a foreseeable time limit for achievement or clear boundaries of acceptable governmental response. For both of these there is a real difficulty in maintaining the enthusiasm and the commitment of their supporters past the initial campaigning stage into the longer haul of maintaining public and political support for half-achieved objectives, without risking disillusionment, despair or boredom. What is needed here is to separate attainable short-term aims from more complicated long-term objectives, and to run campaigns focused upon these intermediate targets. Thus, to 'Stop the Seventies Tour' was an attainable, if only indirectly effective, target in the long struggle to affect relations between Britain and South Africa and to change the structure of South African society, with the strong advantage that it suggested activities to Anti-Apartheid supporters which were appropriate to their different social attitudes and which lifted their morale. Similarly, to focus on the annual aid budget and to measure it against the attainable (though entirely artificial) target of one per cent of GNP on aid provides the aid lobby with a yardstick against which to measure the Government's response to its efforts, and a cycle of activity around which to organise its members.

Almost every group now active is aware that its efforts are aimed at a number of targets. Even the local conservation society concerned to prevent the Council from tearing down its favourite beauty spot is likely to discover that it needs to influence not only the local Council but also the ministerial Department concerned, and that its cause will be served if it can gather the support of local MPs, of the local newspaper, or, even better, of regional radio or television, and of such other local societies and opinion-leaders as it can arouse. A further need is therefore for a group to distinguish as clearly as it can the targets of its activities, and the different approaches needed to win the sympathy of each.

In one way or another the Government must be a central target for most campaigns. Even if its hopes are placed on a private member's bill, a group will still be in need of the favour of the Government Whips to get it through. Much of the reforming legislation passed under the 1960s' Labour Government depended heavily on the provision of additional parliamentary time for its successful passage. Opposition from the responsible Ministry to particular clauses can complicate or even endanger a Bill's passage; parliamentary awareness that the civil servants who will be responsible for implementing an Act welcome its provisions will markedly improve its chances of success. A well-organised group should therefore establish and maintain contact with the Department most concerned with its cause, and should brief itself on the internal organisation and division of responsibilities of the Ministry or Ministries with which it deals. *The British Imperial Calendar and Civil Service List* (HM Stationery Office, annually) for the home civil service, and the *Diplomatic Service List* for the Foreign and Commonwealth Office, will help to give a rough idea of internal departmental responsibilities, if a group has no one amongst its members who knows his way round Whitehall. A well-argued letter supported by information and suggested proposals will serve to establish contact on reasonable lines; if it is signed by, amongst others, an interested MP, it will receive higher-level consideration within the Department and attract a reply from the Minister. Most civil servants welcome the opportunity to justify their actions and to discuss alternatives with interested bodies; indeed, during the Nigerian Civil War the responsible department in the Foreign

Office regretted that the Biafran lobby had made so little effort to put detailed and positive alternative policy proposals to it.

Parliament, as we have already seen, remains for one reason or another a target for most campaigning groups. It is rarely difficult to discover a sympathetic MP; if a new group is sceptical of the help that local MPs may give it, established organisations in its general area concern may offer it helpful advice and introductions. Several directories of Parliament list existing partisan and all-party groups of MPs, from the Airship Association Parliamentary Group to the Friends of Cyclists Group and the Working Group on Education for the Eradication of Colour Prejudice (see for instance *Who Does What in Parliament*, Mitchell & Birt, 2 Cornwall Mansions, Kensington Court, London W8, annually). The more sceptical may prefer Andrew Roth's *The Business Background of MPs* as a guide to members' likely interests, or the latest *Times Book of the House of Commons* (both available in most public libraries) as providing a general picture.

The example of the homosexual law reform legislation should serve to remind activists not to neglect the opportunities presented by the House of Lords. The changed character which the evolution from a predominantly hereditary to a predominantly appointed chamber has given the Lords has raised its prestige and its influence over the last ten years. A Lords debate may often attract less attention in the Press than a Commons debate, but the looser procedure of the Lords makes one easier to obtain; a Lords question to the responsible Ministry may gain a useful response. Furthermore, pressure in the Lords may push the Government into agreeing to re-examine a neglected subject, or even set in train a major enquiry. The experience of the Anti-Discrimination Bill in 1972, talked out in the Commons but reintroduced into the Lords by a Liberal peeress with cross-party support, has so far been instructive. The tone of the Government response was far more amenable upon the Bill's second appearance in the Lords than in its first appearance in the Commons. On its proposers winning the division to introduce the Bill and being granted an unopposed second reading, the matter was referred to a select committee; which guarantees, if not the passage of a Bill, at least a full and open examination of the subject, with interested organisations having the opportunity to present evidence and make proposals. In some respects it may now be fair to say, indeed, that the House of Lords is generally more favourable to progressive legislation than the House of Commons.

The political parties, as already discussed, present another useful target for group activity: for committing an opposition party to implementing a proposal when it regains office, or for persuading the Government to include new ideas in the next Queen's Speech. A motion on the agenda at a Party Conference may help to ventilate an issue, and if debated will gain television time and Press publicity—and perhaps carry its subject into the party programme. Other groups and private organisations may also offer attractive targets, either as valuable potential allies to be won over or as contributors to the wrong which an association is striving to right. Thus the RSPCA, for long officially neutral on hunting, has seen interventions by members of the League against Cruel Sports at successive annual general meetings. Cadbury Schweppes, as a major user of non-returnable bottles, was an early target for the Friends of the Earth; Barclays Bank, with major financial interests in southern Africa, for Anti-Apartheid. In all these cases considerable publicity, and consequent discussion of the issues involved, resulted.

The most difficult targets for group activity are the 'background' elements of bringing pressure to bear on the government: the media and the public themselves. There has been a great deal of discussion in recent years of the 'values' of the media: the subjecting of their assessment of what is 'news', their constant search for novelty, their tendency to reduce issues to personalities, and most of all the concentration of television on colourful or violent action at the expense (or so it is claimed) of more significant but less exciting news. The Stop the Seventy Tour rapidly discovered, according to one of its leaders, that a large but peaceful demonstration 'would only get a brief mention' in the national Press; 'but if it was rowdy and violent, it would get banner headline coverage—with an editorial inside condemning such protests. This made it extremely difficult to justify the continued use of our non-violent strategy.' (Peter Hain, *Don't Play With Apartheid*, 1971, p. 160). The media have themselves been the main objects of pressure from a number of groups, most notably in recent years Mrs Mary Whitehouse's Viewers' and Listeners' Association.

Nevertheless, imperfect as they may be, groups need the media; the Press, radio, and television provide the cheapest and most effective means available of getting their message across to the wider public. Politicians, furthermore, easily mistake Press agitation for aroused public opinion: a "good Press" therefore carries a group's message to the front of governmental and parliamentary attention. So an effective pressure group must cultivate the Press, must do its best to engage the sympathy of reporters and to satisfy their demand for news. For most campaigning issues, this is not too difficult. On one or two questions, such as the Arab-Israeli conflict or some consumer issues, the fear of offending their advertisers may inhibit newspapers' handling of a subject; but these are very few. The media consume news, and the group that provides imaginative stories or appealing pictures has a good chance that they will be used. A great deal of the apparent pro-Biafra bias of the British Press and television during the Nigerian Civil War reflected the greater quantity and superior news-appeal of material provided by the Biafran side rather than a positive commitment. Issues are most easily identified in the popular Press and the popular imagination with personalities; a group therefore needs to provide articulate spokesmen who can 'represent' their cause, as Peter Hain came to represent STST or Mrs Whitehouse the campaign to 'clean up' television.

Governments are sensitive to what they regard as the climate of opinion on particular issues in assessing what policy to adopt or what decision to take. The aid lobby or the Homosexual Law Reform Society needed to change the climate of opinion, or to demonstrate to the government the presence and weight of opinion supporting their cause, in order to strengthen their case. Where the general public is uninformed or uninterested, and the Government not prepared to take up the issue, a long-term effort at public education may be necessary: partly through the medium of Press and television, partly through efforts to change what is taught in the schools. International groups in particular are actively involved in influencing schools and schoolteachers, aiming to catch the imagination and sympathy of the younger generation and to give them a broader view of the world than their elders. Where an immediate crisis or a short-term campaign demands more rapid arousal of public interest, organisations such as Shelter or Christian Aid have effectively used advertisements to shock their public into awareness; but both would probably see such short-term efforts against the background of a longer-term educational campaign.

The tactics a group adopts to gain its objectives, and the weapons it uses to advance its cause, must of course be related to the character of its aims and its assessment of the obstacles to their achievement. Respectability and reputation are valuable weapons for a group with not too radical aims, giving it easy access to government departments, to parliamentarians and to mass media alike. A reputation for reliable and accurate information, particularly if not easily available elsewhere, is particularly valuable: it provides material for the Press, for parliamentary speeches, and for use in lobbying the Government. DIG's careful efforts to collect material on the policies towards the disabled of other European governments provided persuasive arguments to Ministers and civil servants; HLRS's careful case studies helped to sway parliamentary opinion. Amnesty International and the Minority Rights Group rely to a considerable extent on the accuracy of the information they collect, and the publicity their reports receive, for the influence they aim at.

A body of supporting MPs, preferably drawn from more than one party, is an invaluable weapon to a group which knows how to make use of Parliament. MPs are professionally concerned with a whole range of issues; they therefore appreciate, and are likely to make most use of, short briefing material which is selectively distributed to those most prepared to use it, rather than lengthy and detailed studies sent indiscriminately to sympathetic and unsympathetic members. Pressure group material distributed to MPs is competing with a mass of propaganda from foreign governments and leaflets from other organisations; the Study of Parliament Group's *The Member of Parliament and His Information* (by Anthony Barker and Michael Rush, 1970) provides an instructive picture of members' attitudes to this postbag. Circulation of material to MPs needs therefore to be reinforced by personal contacts with sympathetic members in order to be effective.

A certain sophistication in identifying and addressing one's audience is apparent in a number of organisations' efforts to win over opinion inside and outside the government. Establishment opinion is most easily won over by respectable groups with established names on their letterheads, while students, for instance, are as often repelled as attracted by such an image. Many groups have therefore worked through what are to a greater or lesser extent 'front' organisations. The European Movement at present sponsors fifteen, from the Committee of Student European Associations to the Conservative Group for Europe; the Biafran lobby and STST created or supported the creation of separate committees for similar reasons. Through such means the respectable parent body can retain its reputation for moderation with the Government, while its student affiliate takes part in direct action.

Direct action itself has retained its appeal and its usefulness for pressure groups, even though the opportunities for access to the Government have widened so vastly since the eighteenth century. It serves as a last resort, a final sanction for groups which have failed to obtain satisfaction through more conventional channels, from trade unions to Women's Lib. It catches public attention, if not always public sympathy, and demonstrates strength of feeling or breadth of support. As significantly, it serves to give group members a feeling of being active, and so raises and maintains morale, or even provides a sense of immediate achievement. Activity at the local level, through branches throughout the country, can provide impressive evidence of the extent of the support which a cause can command. The ability of the aid lobby to make representations to MPs in their own constituencies, to raise their cause in local newspapers, and to mount a sign-in in churches throughout the country, contributed a great deal to the seriousness with which the Government treated its representations. For a group which is asking the Government to spend more money on its chosen cause the ability to raise money can itself be an effective means of pressure and a source of achievement for its members. The £8 million the organisations of the aid lobby were raising every year provided irrefutable evidence that some of the public were prepared to spend money on development; the sponsored walks and other money-raising activities of Shelter helped to strengthen the commitment of those who took part in them.

All six of the organisations described in this study are recent groups; only the Homosexual Law Reform Society, as a political pressure group, existed before 1960. Has the environment of pressure group activity changed much in the past ten years? Certainly a new generation of pressure groups now exists, covering in many cases what are effectively new issues: environmental pollution, race relations, the threat to privacy from the growth of administration and the advance of technology. Some of the problems with which they deal are the unforeseen by-products of social improvement and medical or economic advance: the break-up of the old family unit as society becomes more mobile, the greater expectation of life, the new pockets of poverty which the alleviation of mass poverty has left behind. The new, predominantly middle-class leadership of many of these groups reflects the educational revolution of the last two generations: no longer are groups dominated, as so often twenty years ago, by the familiar figures of 'the great and the good' or of the 'lilac establishment' who could be found in their rival ranks signing letters to the *Times,* but more often by a much wider group of professionals, teachers, academics from the expanded universities, and others capable and confident of lobbying MPs on equal terms or dealing with civil servants or Press reporters.

What may be new is not so much the tactics of these groups, which are mostly well tried and familiar, or their aims, as the extent to which the activities have in the past ten years come to invade what had previously been regarded as the province of the political parties. The membership of all three conventional political parties has fallen in the past decade, from perhaps between three and three and a half million in 1960 to perhaps two million in 1970; the total was probably higher still in the mid-fifties. (Some figures are given in *The British General Election of 1970* by D. E. Butler & Michael Pinto-Duschinsky, Chapter XI.) It is tempting to suggest, though the evidence does not support more than a suggestion, that many people who ten years before would have been attracted to campaign for their beliefs through the medium of a political party are now more easily attracted to a cause group, be it the Child Poverty Action Group or the Society for Individual Freedom. Certainly the emergence of new organisations alongside the established pressure groups of British politics has served to involve a great many new people in political activity at a time when activity through parties has been declining, and as such has contributed in itself to the democratic process.

There are many remaining imperfections in the British democratic process which group activities have neither alleviated nor solved. The groups themselves are often internally not very democratic—though the competition of rival bodies helps to maintain an open debate. The resources available to groups, particularly in terms of finance, are often disproportionate to the importance of the cause they promote; though it is often not the wealthiest groups which are the most successful. The membership and leadership of organised groups is still predominantly drawn from the middle-class, and has largely failed to draw in working-class activity as working-class membership of the Labour Party has declined. But in a fairly free society, with a fairly free Press and a fairly open Government, the activities of pressure groups do serve to raise and to debate issues which the political parties have neglected or preferred not to discuss—such as the pollution of the environment, or the case for or against going into the European Community. They serve also to gain satisfaction for groups of concerned people who would have little opportunity for influencing their fellows or their political governors on their own. The potential activist needs patience and perseverance in considering how to campaign—he might do well to remember that the Anti-Slavery Society still exists, and is still uncovering cases of slavery in parts of the world. But he should find sufficient evidence of other campaigns' successes, often without large resources or initial patronage, to encourage him to try.

# FURTHER READING

*Parliament and Conscience,* Peter G. Richards, London, 1970.
   This is an interesting study of social reform legislation, covering capital punishment, homosexuality, abortion, theatre censorship, divorce, and Sunday entertainment.

*Capital Punishment and British Politics,* James B. Christoph, London, 1962.

'The Minister's Line: or, the M4 comes to Berkshire' by Roy Gregory.
   Two articles in *Public Administration* for Summer and Autumn 1967, covering the planning process and the protests.

*Abortion Law Reformed,* Madeleine Simms & Keith Hindell, London, 1970.

*The Clean-up TV Campaign,* Mary Whitehouse, London, 1967.

*Influencing Voters,* Richard Rose, London, 1967.
   This is an academic study of party and interest group propaganda campaigns, and the obstacles they face in getting their message across to the voters.

*Communication and Political Power,* Lord Windlesham, London, 1966
   This contains an interesting essay on the contrasting approaches of the pro- and anti-EEC pressure groups during the first Conservative application, 1961–63.

*Anonymous Empire,* S. E. Finer, 2nd Edition, London, 1966.
   This is a straighforward introduction to pressure group activity in Britain, with examples drawn from campaigns in the early sixties.